# LOOK MA, NO HANDS, NO LEGS EITHER

THIS STORY IS MORE THAN A MEMOIR
THIS IS A TRUE INSPIRATIONAL STORY OF OVERCOMING
THE ODDS AND LIVING LIFE TO IT'S FULLNESS.

KENT BELL

**LOOK MA, NO HANDS, NO LEGS EITHER**



*iUniverse books may be ordered through booksellers or by contacting:*

*iUniverse*
*1663 Liberty Drive*
*Bloomington, IN 47403*
*www.iuniverse.com*
*1-800-Authors (1-800-288-4677)*



*ISBN: 978-1-4917-3689-0 (sc)*
*ISBN: 978-1-4917-3690-6 (e)*

*Library of Congress Control Number: 2014912036*

*Printed in the United States of America.*

*iUniverse rev. date: 8/27/2014*

THIS BOOK IS DEDICATED TO EVERYBODY WHO HAS HELPED ME THROUGH MY JOURNEY IN LIFE---

MATTHEW 18:9- IT IS BETTER FOR THEE TO ENTER INTO LIFE HALT OR MAIMED, RATHER THAN HAVING TWO HANDS OR TWO FEET TO BE CAST INTO EVERLASTING FIRE. (KJV)

# CONTENTS

# FOREWARD

The following stories are from coaches at The University of North Florida, Jacksonville, Florida.

Coach Driscoll's story when he met Kent.

> My first contact with Kent was when he sent an email to discuss referees at home venues. He mentioned, "don't worry you don't have to physically feed me."
>
> I knew at that moment he was passionate about hoops and extremely comfortable in his own skin.
>
> Later we met in my office door way. I looked down and found myself resting my foot on one of his wheels. I quickly apologized and asked for forgiveness when he responded, "Coach, relax it's no big deal."
>
> No arms or legs and all I'm worried about is zone offense? Really!!
>
> If you can't be motivated and moved to get

better after reading this book you need a lot of help!

Urgency Never Fails

Stay Blessed!!!

Coach Matthew Driscoll
Men's Basketball Coach
The University of North Florida

Coach Mary Tappmeyer:

I first met Kent through our former Sports Information Director, Bonnie Senappe. She is a huge practical joker, so when she told me she had hired a scoreboard operator from the Midwest who had worked at Indiana/Purdue University, Indianapolis, Indiana, I was very excited. She said he was very good but there was something a little different about him. He had no arms or legs.

I assumed she was pulling a joke on me so I said, okay. The first time I met him was on a game day, so I went up to introduce myself and welcome him to the Osprey family. Imagine my surprise when I stuck out my hand to shake hands with him and I realized Bonnie had been serious! I quickly patted him on the top of his head to welcome him.

It is now a home game ritual that I always perform. I always pat the top of his head for luck. He inspires me with his passion for the game of basketball and positive attitude about life. I have never met such an inspirational person. I believe he has never let his situation affect his outlook on life. I count him as one of my blessings & lessons about life.

Head Coach, Mary Tappmeyer,
Women's Basketball Team
The University of North Florida
Jacksonville, Florida

Coach Nancy Miller:

Kent has been an integral member of our UNF basketball family for almost 20 years. Game day wouldn't be complete if I didn't see Kent sitting court side at the scorer's table and be able to give him my "high five" - which between Kent and me is a head pat! He is a constant inspiration to me and a reminder on a daily basis that life is to be LIVED with passion, joy, and a good sense of humor! He is a good friend, a great scoreboard operator and a lifelong Osprey. It is an honor to know him.

Assistant Coach, Nancy Miller,
Women's Basketball
University of North Florida, Jacksonville, FL

# INTRODUCTION

Hello. My name is Kenton Ray Bell. I am forty three years old and I am disabled. I was born with Congenital Quadrarhyteamelia, in layman's terms--no arms or legs.

This is the story of my life thus far. When I had an idea for my book I did not want it to be just me writing about myself. When I read autobiographies, they're too self-serving & over-melodramatic to me.

Not this time. Sure, I'll be doing the writing for the most part, but in this book you will read thoughts and feelings from my family and friends who really know me.

This will not be your typical book about a person with a disability. Some are either too sweet or too depressing. This will be both.

Some of it is funny, depressing, anger-filled, caring, but most of all, the book is about how I have adjusted and embraced my disability and how others see and feel about me. So, turn the page and let's begin this journey.

*Mom and Dad*

# 1

# Born Into A Military Family

*Dad's Retirement-US ARMY*
*Ft. Harrison Indiana*
*Brother Vic, Dad, Mom, brother Danny, Kent and sister Kimberly,*

According to my mom, the actual events are blurry because right after I was delivered, the doctor sedated her, thinking she will have a crazy episode when she realized she had a child with no working parts. Little did he know that I would be the one driving her crazy.

The one thing she did recall before being sedated was that the nurse who was an African-American turned ash white when I was being delivered. More details of the delivery will be told later in the book.

My dad went into my mom's room to tell her what happened. He also told her that he and the doctor had been talking about where to bury me because the doctor did not think I'd live through the week. Should I be buried in Virginia or Indiana, where both sides of my family reside? My mom spoke up and said, "Don't talk like that. He's not going to die." That scenario would repeat itself several times in my life.

Needless to say, after a six-week stay in the ICU, my parents were finally able to bring me home to my two brothers, Victor and Daniel.

There were no instructions at the time on how to raise a child without any arms or legs. My mom is working on that book as I'm writing this one.

She just decided to raise me as "normal" as possible, along with my siblings. I put normal in quotation marks because if you were raised in the military as I was, you would know nothing is quite "normal".

I stated that my Mom made the decision on how to raise me. When it came time for an important decision, mom was the one who made it. Dad's job was to serve his country and protect us all. Up until 1993, Dad was not much of a family man. He would try to do family things, but that evil demon called alcohol would mostly ruin stuff. The most important thing to understand is that my dad would be the first one to agree with me.

When my Dad was not drinking, he was the nicest, funniest man I ever met. Unfortunately, from 1965 to 1993, I only saw that side of him maybe 10 percent. The other 90 percent of the time, alcohol would turn him into a belligerent, evil person.

The one thing that dad taught us was that we can fight amongst ourselves, but if anyone outside the family tries to hurt a family member, we protect the family member as a group and then we seek out the perpetrator as a group.

You may have heard that children who have military parents are referred to as "Army Brats". You may also have heard that, because the families keep moving from state to state, the parents will spoil their children to help in the adjustments brought on by the constantly changing environments.

Not my family. We were far from being spoiled. My dad never made much money because he was an enlisted man, not an officer.

The only thing in our house that was spoiled was either milk or cheese.

Some kids found it difficult to constantly keep moving. On my behalf, I believe the military was an enhancement. Here is a list of places I have lived since I was born:

1. Ft. Belvoir, Virginia
2. Rensselaer, Indiana
3. Lakehurst, New Jersey
4. Chicago, Illinois
5. Ft. Rucker, Alabama
6. Indianapolis, Indiana
7. Newport News, Virginia
8. Fairbanks, Alaska
9. Mt. Clemens, Michigan
10. Indianapolis, Indiana
11. Lexington, Kentucky
12. Indianapolis, Indiana
13. Kingsland, Georgia
14. Jacksonville, Florida. (currently reside)

Because we lived in all of those places, we were exposed to different environments, persons and cultures. For me, it was a special bonus, especially from Alaska to Indiana listed number 10.

You see, since we lived on military bases in most of those places, my siblings had to go to school on the bases where they were around children who constantly moved also. As for myself, I went to schools inside the cities.

They would bus me into the communities and my friends were children who were born and raised in their towns, so I experienced each culture from my school friends.

Since we constantly moved, this also improved my friendship- making skills.

Children in military families have two options when it comes to friendships:

1. Make friends as quickly as possible before you move or
2. Don't make friends at all.

I chose number one. I have never allowed my disability to become a hindrance in obtaining friends. If I saw a kid who was hesitant to approach me because of my disability, I would approach them by saying, "It's ok, your arms and legs will not fall off if we're friends."

The most difficult move was in 1973. We moved from Newport News, Virginia to Fairbanks, Alaska.

My parents had this bright idea, instead of flying from Virginia to Alaska, they said, "let's drive cross- country in our station wagon so the kids can see the country and be educated."

Remember the Brady Bunch Show where Mr. and Mrs. Brady decided to load six children, a dog and housekeeper into a station wagon for a cross country trip? Apparently, my parents did not watch those episodes.

Here's a summary of the trip.

Day 1: Get up at 6:00 a.m Begin to load Station Wagon. Dad makes announcement, "Better go to the bathroom now, because we're not stopping until sunset". Children in the back fighting about where to sit so we can make goofy faces at other drivers and semi trucks. Dad starts drinking beer. Mom yells at him for drinking.

Dad yelling at kids to pipe down or he'll stop the car to whoop us. Then there were kids whining to go to the bathroom after twelve hours.

Then we checked into a hotel.

Day 2: Repeat Day 1.

Day 3: Repeat Days 1-2.

Day 4: Repeat Days 1-3 until youngest child gets motion sickness on dangerous mountain road which prompts dad to say, "Hang your head out the back window to throw up."

Day 5: Repeat Days 1-4 without motion sickness, arriving at destination, which prompts major family decision. When we move back to the mainland, we're flying because we were sick and tired of each other. Family unanimously agrees.

So, what have we learned in this chapter?

1. Not all military children are "Army brats",
2. Moving constantly can be fun and educational at least for the children.
3. Never take a five-day trip with four kids in a station wagon.

Chapter two will focus on my relationship with my dad. I'll do this by mostly talking about the conversations he and

I had. There are a few situations where our relationship was so strained that from 1981-86 I only spoke to him once. Some of it is not pretty, but it needs to be said. If the problems we experienced had never occurred, the reunion would not have been so great and I beg each and every one of you who has a similar relationship with your parent to try and patch things up before you lose them. Luckily, I got that chance before he died in 2004.

*Mom, Dad, Danny and Victor*

# 2

## Conversations with My Dad

This chapter for me will be the most difficult one to write. As stated at the end of chapter one, from 1965 to 1993 my dad and I had a very rocky relationship due to him drinking. Actually, it wasn't the drinking itself it was the effect of alcohol that changed his personality without warning. Have you heard the phrase walking on eggshells? That was my family when my dad was drinking.

My dad's name is Everett Marshall Bell. He was born in a little country town called Fair Oaks Indiana. His mom Margaret and father George Bell, sister Shirley, sister Barbara and brother Dick. I'll go into detail about my grandmother, aunts and uncle later in the book.

I cannot write about my grandpa Bell because he died before I was born.

Apparently, from what has been told to me Grandpa Bell was also a heavy drinker. He also could not control his temper when drinking. You guessed it there's a pattern.

Dad was thrown out of high school because he hit the principal in defending his sister. According to my dad and Aunt Barbara, my dad saw the principal slap her for smoking. My dad went up to him and punched him. When Grandpa Bell heard about it he gave dad two choices, 1: move out and get a job or 2: go into the military. My dad chose the Army.

My dad was stationed at Ft. Harrison in Indianapolis,

Indiana where he met the one true love of his life - Bobbie Jean Yates. When dad was young he literally looked like the 50's version of Elvis Presley, including the smirk. According to mom he was also sweet, caring, funny, and swept her off her feet.

On August, 25th 1961 they got married. My dad was then stationed to Anchorage Alaska where both of my brothers were born. My mom said during those times dad would either be at work or in the NCO Club. The longer he stayed in the Army, the more he drank.

On March 27th 1964 Good Friday, Anchorage was hit by a devastating earthquake that measured 9.2 on the Richter scale.

To date it was the largest earthquake recorded in North America. According to the Anchorage Daily News, The seismic waves could be felt as far away as South Africa.

Mom was at home with her two sons Victor and Daniel. Dad was flying in the Huey helicopter when everything occurred. The pilot was trying to land at the precise time of the earthquake. At that moment they did not know what was happening, but as they tried to land, the earth started opening up. The pilot managed to land the helicopter. We found out later that dad had been sitting on a tubular tank they were transporting and that is when we believe he was exposed to radiation. The radiation may have been the cause of my birth defects, but we could never prove it.

After they landed, dad went home to get the family and transported them to a designated place for families. Then he and fellow soldiers went around town and the Alaskan villages rescuing people and taking photos of the damage.

In all only 131 people died in the quake from Alaska to California. Only 9 of those were directly attributed to the quake. The remaining 122 people died in tsunamis off the coasts of

Alaska, Canada, Washington, Oregon & California. As I have stated a couple of times, when something major happened in the family we always managed to rally around each other.

Then in the latter part of 1964 my dad was stationed in Ft. Belvoir, Virginia where I was born. Then in 1966 we moved to Rensselaer Indiana where my sister Kimberly was born.

During my infancy, I do not remember much interaction between my father and I. Now I do remember when I was four years old the following happened.

The place was at Ft. Rucker, Alabama. Dad bought a motorcycle and it appeared to be the biggest event on the block. Everyone took turns riding it. After my siblings had their turn riding on the cycle with dad, my mom actually agreed to allow dad to take me for a ride. Dad sat me on the gas tank and put his right arm around me while he would drive using his left hand. At first, I was enjoying it until dad jumped the curb. When we landed my butt hit the gas cap and pain shot up my butt to my spine. I remembered mom yelling at him. "You bring him back here! You're going to kill him!" Needless to say, I have never been on a motorcycle since and I will never get on one again.

Dad went away for a few years to fight in Vietnam. At the time I did not understand why my daddy wasn't home. Mom tried to explain but I was too young to grasp it. I do remember my dad coming home from the war……..

We were living in Indianapolis, Indiana in an apartment complex. Mom was upstairs getting dressed. The doorbell rang and my oldest brother Vic opened the door. Outside the door was a guy dressed in military uniform holding flowers. Vic yells upstairs to mom the following phrase: "Mommy! There's a man in a Army uniform with flowers for you!" Mom flies down the stairs, through the screen door and hugs and kisses the man. Luckily, it was dad.

I did not know it was dad because he was gone for years in another country. After returning from Vietnam, I remembered the first conversation I had alone with dad. I was lying on the bed as he was putting on his shirt. On my dad's left side of his chest there was a slit going sideways. I asked my dad what it was. This is what he told me.

"It's a bayonet wound. I was in a foxhole when the North Vietnamese soldiers decided to attack. One of the North Vietnamese Soldiers was on the edge of the foxhole pointing his bayonet at me. I shot and killed him but as he fell into the foxhole, the SOB's bayonet stabbed me."

That was the only time that my dad ever talked to me about his experience in Vietnam. Looking back, I'm kind of glad he didn't talk more about it.

The next conversation I remember between my dad and I was when I was eight years old. My dad was drinking a beer. I wondered what his fascination was drinking it. I thought to myself "it must taste pretty good for my dad to drink it all the time." So, I asked my dad if I could taste it.

Without mom looking he gave me a sip. It was AWFUL. I looked at my dad and went: "EEEWW! That's nasty how can you drink it?" My dad responded: "It's an acquired taste." I told him, "Well, I don't want to acquire it."

Even though he never admitted it, I believe that was his reason for giving me a taste. If I tasted it and hated it I would not drink it when I grew up. I have never drank beer since. I said beer because we will get to my partying days later.

One soft spot my father had, was for animals. He was especially fond of dogs. Wherever we moved as soon as we were settled my dad would begin a search for a pet "for the kids". I put that in quotation marks because looking back I believe dad wanted a dog as much as we did. Dad tolerated cats because mom loves them. But he preferred a dog anytime.

It didn't matter how smart the dog was, if my dad saw a cute puppy with big paws it was coming to our house. Dad understood if a puppy has big paws it would grow up to be a big dog for rough housing and security. No wiener or yip yip dogs in our house.

One particular dog was a German shepherd named Paul. Ask anyone in my family and they will tell you Paul was the greatest dog we ever had. He was a beautiful golden brown. He was intelligent and kind to children. He would lie down beside me and he would let me use him as a pillow. My siblings were small enough and he was big enough that they could ride him like a pony. Well, one day my dad had some bad news.

The landlady who was the stereotypical "The cat lady" told my dad that her cats were being killed and she was accusing our dog of killing her cats. She told my dad either get rid of the dog or move. Needless to say my mom and dad argued about that and I remember my dad telling mom: " You think I want to get rid of the dog? I love that dog as much as the kids do!"

After we cried and gave away our dog the landlady's cats kept getting killed she discovered too late that instead of our sweet dog killing her cats it was our next door neighbor's dog. So I have a special message to that landlady.

If you or your family member I.E. mother, sister, cousin was an apartment manager in Newport News Va. in 1972. And you made a family get rid of their dog because you or your relative falsely accused our dog of killing those cats. YOU OWE ME A GERMAN SHEPHERD!" I want retribution.

Now, let me tell you about the time my dad saved my life. It's true. Now it wasn't as harrowing as Vietnam or later you will read about saving my sister, but he did save my life. I was 10 years old. I developed a strange stomach virus.

I couldn't keep solid food down. Everything I ate came right back up. The only thing that seemed to stay down, were those red, white and blue rocket popsicles. I was ten years old and having to eat popsicles made me happy.

After seven days of eating popsicles got old and my stomach was shrinking.

My dad was cooking dinner. My dad was a fantastic cook. He cooked things such as fried green tomatoes, fried chicken, polish sausage, fried potatoes and Hungarian goulash.

On this particular day he cooked fried chicken, mashed potatoes and biscuits. I didn't like mashed potatoes, but my dad, without saying a word, sat me up to the table. He took a fork and put a small piece of chicken some mashed potatoes and a piece of biscuit on it and put it in my mouth. With my dad, you don't questions, you just do it.

I ate the food while my dad nervously looked at me. After I swallowed the food, my dad asked me, "Well?" I waited a few seconds, looked at my stomach and nothing bad was going on so I said: "I think it's not coming back up. I feel fine." My dad smiled and asked me if I wanted more. I said yes. So, that's how my dad saved my life.

Let's fast forward to fall of 1980. This was the funniest conversation I ever had with him. It was a Sunday afternoon. My dad and I were watching football and for a rare occasion the games were boring. My dad was flipping the channels when he stopped on a religious channel featuring Tele-Evangelist Ernest Angley.

Preacher Angley was from Dayton Ohio with a soft Southern accent and a really bad toupee. Brother Angley was walking with God. Here was his message in a southern drawl :

"My Friends, Sinners, walk like their walking on egg shells. But I'll tell you my friends, I'm walking on the footy prints of Gawd." That's right readers he said footy prints. I looked at my dad and I could see by his expression he knew I was going to ask him a question that he had knew he could not answer.

So, here is the next scenario:

Me talking: "Dad,

Dad: "Yes son…."

Me: "What are footy prints?"

Dad (chuckling): "I have no idea, ask your mother."

Mom got home from shopping and I asked her what are footy prints? My mom thought I was crazy and I had to re-enact the scene for her.

She looked at my dad and he says: "Kent's telling you the truth. I told him I didn't know what footy prints are and he would have to ask you because you go to church."

Well, mom said footy prints are just footprints. Luckily, later that evening they re-ran that sermon and my mom saw it and it has become my routine at family gatherings imitating Ernest Angley. My mom even bought me a powder blue suit like the reverend wore to give my skit full effect.

This was one of the funniest times I remember.

Now I will tell you my worst memory.

Fast forward to October 1981…

During the summer of 81, my parents separated, I almost died of a urinary tract infection and the only good thing to occurred that year was my nephew Christopher was born.

It was a Monday night that to this day brings nightmares to me. It started nice and quiet. I was in my room watching Monday Night Football. My sister was downstairs looking after our nephew babysitting. Dad had moved up to Rensselaer, Indiana.

Brother Victor was married and my sister and I were watching his baby. My brother Daniel was in college, and my mom was out.

At approximately 9:30 p.m. the front door flew open and my dad was yelling “Where is she!?” My sister ran up the stairs to tell my dad to be quiet because the baby was trying to sleep. My dad started yelling and saying crazy things to my sister and calling her a whore and saying that my sister was not really his daughter because my dad was accusing mom of having affairs while he was in Vietnam.

Later I had learned he had been threatening to burn down the house with us in it.

Imagine yourself at the age of fifteen and your own dad is calling you these wicked names and saying you’re not his child. My sister ran into her room crying. It gets worse.

About 15 minutes later my sister comes out of her room and comes into mine. Tears all down her face, she says: “Kent, I’m having trouble breathing. I just took a bottle of pills and I can’t breathe.”

My first reaction was denial. I did not and would not believe my sister would overdose. I told my sister to “go open the front door, take a few deep breaths. Dad was just being a jerk.”

Well, she went to the front door, opened it for a few minutes then closed it, walked downstairs to where the baby was.

The next thing I heard confirmed my worst fears. I heard my dad yelling: “Stop shaking like that! Stop rolling your eyes to the back of your head! Stop Convulsing! D###mit! Stop it Kim!” My first thought was “F###, she really did it! She really overdosed!”

My dad ran upstairs and was asking me what to do. I told him: “Call 911, tell them your daughter overdosed on pills and give them our address.” Dad called them and was giving the operator the information when all of a sudden he stopped and said: "It's too late she's gone."

He dropped the phone and collapsed. I rolled out of my room pissed off and started yelling at my dad: "G## d##mit Dad! My sister is not going to die because of your f###ing bull####! You get your f###ing ass downstairs and bring her up here!"

My dad got up, went downstairs and carried her up to the living room. He was asking me what to do. All I could remember was watching an episode of Emergency where David Cassidy overdoses and they showed how to treat it. I told my dad to stand her up, keep her moving. As time was passing she became more and more listless. As a last ditch effort, I told my dad to stick his finger down her throat to force her to throw up. Little did I know there's a dangerous part to doing that.

As my dad was trying to force her to throw up, there was a knock on the door. I saw the flashing lights out the window, so I knew it was the paramedics. I moved to the left side of the stairs so the paramedics can get straight to my sister.

My dad and I both yelled: "Come in and up the stairs!" The front door flew opened and a police officer drew his gun and instead of pointing the gun straight up the stairs he pointed it to the left which was exactly aimed at me. I closed my eyes and I asked God to make the policeman pull the trigger. I told God if he should take someone take me because my sister would have a better chance of success than I would. When the policeman saw I was not a threat, he apologized and put his gun in the holster. I was really upset now because I thought that God made his decision and he was taking Kim. I rolled in my room bawling because I was sure she wasn't going to make it.

The policeman came into my room. He apologized for pointing his gun at me, then he asked me what happened. I accepted his apology then I told him everything that happened that evening. While I was talking to the police, the paramedics were scrambling around looking for the pill bottle so they could administer the correct anti-dote. I just yelled out, "I don't know. Just look for an empty bottle."

They found it. It was a prescription of benedryl to stop swelling of mosquito bites. She just got the prescription that day and now the whole bottle was empty.

After they found the bottle and was administering the anti-dote, one of the paramedics came in my room to ask me what happened. I told him everything. When I got to the part about having my dad force her to throw up the paramedic stopped me and said: "Sometimes that might do worse damage." I asked how?

Paramedic responded: "If the drug/medication is acid based such as LSD, when a person throws it up, the acid from the drug can burn the internal stomach and can hypothetically do worse harm."

Now, I'm really worried that I may have accidentally caused worse damage. The paramedic concluded: "In this case, it looks like you did the right thing." Well, my mom got home and saw everything going on but did not know the true story until now. She jumped into her car and headed to the hospital. Vic and Gina returned home to get the baby. Everybody left for the hospital except me. Everything happened so fast, nobody thought to put me in my wheelchair and take me.

There I was, 16 yrs old, disabled, watching my sister's life fading away because of my dad's bull#### drinking. I literally thought of rolling down the stairs in hopes of breaking my neck so I would die. I cried so much that night I did not have the energy to do it.

The next morning I awoke to my mom washing dishes. I

came out of my room. Dad was sitting in a chair with his head in his hands. I asked mom for some iced tea.

When my dad heard me he got up and started walking towards me. I stopped and glared at him. At that moment my dad was my worst enemy. Because of him my sister is in the hospital dying.

If I had even one arm I would have done my best to try and kill him. That's how mad I was.

Apparently, my glare gave that message to him because he ran outside crying. My sister kept going in and out of consciousness.

Mom got me ready for school, put me on the bus and headed back to the hospital where she stayed most of the time.

I attempted to call the hospital from my high school to get a report. Even after telling the stupid nurse I was the brother of the patient she refused to tell me. Three days went by without a report.

Finally, on the third day, after school, I'm home by myself, The bus driver helped me into the house and put the phone where I can reach it. After the driver leaves the phone rings and I answered it:

This was the conversation:

Me: Hello?

Scratchy voice: Kent, this is Kim

Me: Kim who?

Kim: Your sister Kim.

Me (crying tears of joy): Kim? You're alive, thank God you're alive!

Kim: I don't know why you did it, but thanks for saving my life.

Me: You're quite welcome but please promise me not to do that again.

Kim: I promise

Years later, I asked my sister how she knew that it was me who saved her life. Kim said: I heard everything you told dad." I said: "But, you were unconscious." she replied: "I still heard you."

That event in 1981 put a deep separation between my dad and I. Because of what he did I chose to speak to my dad only once from 1981-86. If he called me, I refused to answer it. If he sent me a card, I'd throw it away without opening it. The only time in that five year period I chose to speak to him was in 1983 to invite him to my high school graduation.

It was one statement: "You are my dad. I do want you to come to my graduation. However, there is one condition. No drinking. I told mom if I smell alcohol on you I'm authorizing her to take you home." He agreed. Sure enough when graduation went, my dad was sober.

After that major event, you'd think there would not be anything to repair the damage. For years I would have agreed with you. But on July 29th 1993 that all changed.

Two days earlier, my sister's fiance was murdered at a local restaurant drive-thru and died. On one hand, it was horrible. But, that event galvanized our family and began the process of healing.

But, not in the usual theory of life is too short. No, this was on a much deeper level.

On July 29th, my dad called my mom's house to talk to me. Here is that conversation.

Dad: "How is she?"

Me: "Under the circumstances, ok I guess."

Dad: "Kent, I don't know if I can handle this."

Me: "Handle what?"

Dad: "When we get to the funeral home my little girl is going to come running to me crying 'He's gone daddy, He's gone.' and I don't know if I can stand seeing my little girl crushed."

Me: "I understand. For the last two days, I've seen it and every time I see her cry it feels like a knife stabbing me in the heart over and over again."

Dad: "I've not been much of a father to you kids. I don't know what to do."

Me: (long Pause) "I'm not going to give you some Ozzie & Harriet Answer. You're right you've not been much of a father but here is a chance to start. When Kim runs to you crying "he's gone daddy, he's gone" here is what you do. When she puts her arms around you and starts crying, no matter how much it hurts, you hug her and you keep on hugging her until she pulls away from you."

Dad: "I don't know if I can."

Me: "For your daughter, you have to do it. She needs her daddy, and like it or not, you are it.

First, a couple of thoughts were running in my head during our phone conversation.

1. Why was he asking me for advice? He was the supposed adult.
2. Why ask me for advice on how to be a father when I don't have children? He could have talked to either one of my brothers who have kids. But on this occasion, he decided to speak to me. I'm thankful he did.

We went to the funeral home. Everything happened exactly as we talked on the phone. As soon as we entered, here comes Kim running towards dad crying, "He's gone daddy, he's gone."

As she was crying, for the first time in my life, I saw real heartbreak and pain in my father's eyes. His knees began to buckle, but he took a deep breath, straightened his knees, hugged his daughter tighter, brushed her hair back and kissed her on top of the head saying. "I know, I'm sorry, I love you Kim." He held on.

A few minutes passed and after Kim pulled away, my dad went outside to smoke. I followed him.

Dad: "That hurt. That really hurts."

Me: "I know dad. I saw it in your eyes. But, you did it. You were there for her and you did not back down. You were a ROCK for her. Today, I'm proud to say you acted like a dad. Like our dad. I love you."

From that moment until the day he died in 2004, dad and I did everything possible to patch things up. I would call him, he would call me. I'd go to his house to visit. He would visit me.

He started to slow down his drinking and his temper.

Later, dad would tell me stories about him and mom dating. One story in particular:

## PROM NIGHT 1961

Dad: "I was driving my convertible. The top was down. Your mother saw some friends of hers, stood up in the car to wave at them and as I turned the corner, the pizza box slid into her seat and when she sat down she sat in the pizza with her prom dress on.

According to mom, when she stood up, he put the box in her seat. When confronted with this he slyly said "I did not." I asked him, "Did you turn so sharply that when the pizza box slid into mom's seat it also forced the box to open? My dad laughed and said: You're too smart son."

*Dad, Myself, Vic*

## MIRACLE- DAD QUIT DRINKING

In April 2002, the first of two miracles occurred. My dad stopped drinking completely. He had a health issue and he finally said: "I'm sick and tired of being sick and tired."

My dad did not gradually reduce his drinking, I mean he went from drinking a case (24 cans) a day to zero.

When he told me he was drinking a case a day I asked: "How?

There's only 24 hours in a day but you were drinking an average of one can per hour every day?" He couldn't answer.

He attempted to stop drinking in 1981 but that lasted one month. So, when he said he was going to stop in 2002 I was skeptical that it would last. He made it through the first month, then two months. In the third month he came down to Florida for a visit. He came to my work.

I had just received an award for being the top advocate for disabled rights in the state of Florida and received a plaque.

99% of the time I would give the plaque to my mom because she would deserve it. But, I decided this one goes to dad.

Here is what I told him.

"Dad, Kim, Vic and I agreed that you were the hardest working person we know. No matter what shape you were in the night before, every day, you'd get up at 5:00 a.m. get dressed in military uniform and performed your duty.

Judging by your Commendations and your certificates you did a dang good job. Therefore, dad because this plaque symbolizes my work ethic, I'm giving it to you because you showed me by example of what hard work and dedication can do."

My dad cried and we hugged.

Fast forward to June 16th 2003. Little did we know at the time this would be my dad's last birthday and Father's Day. Two weeks earlier my mom, step dad and I had gone up to see him. My dad still had not drunk a drop in fourteen months and going strong. My dad was the perfect host. Getting coffee, mingling, and joking.

As we were heading back to Florida, my mom said to me: "Kent, since your dad stopped drinking he has turned back into the man I originally fell in love with."

On June 16th 2003, I decided that I was going to do something special for him. I called him with a dual purpose.

Me: "Happy Birthday and Father's day dad."

Dad: "Thanks son."

Me: "Dad, I don't have gifts or cards for you."

Dad: "You know you don't have to get me anything. Just as long as you love me, that's all I need."

Me: "I do love you dad. Not many kids can say this about their dad, but, Vic, Kim and I can say this about you.

Dad: "What?"

Me: "To us dad, you are a two time hero."

Dad: "What do you mean two time hero?"

Me: " Well dad, 1st you are a war hero. Even though you probably didn't want to go to Vietnam, you went, to protect those people and you did it so we can have food on the plate and a roof over our heads. The second time, you did something even I didn't think you could do."

Dad: "What's that?"

Me: "You stopped drinking. You did it on your own. You did it completely. To stop drinking like you did shows strength and courage beyond compare.

For that, in my eyes you are a true hero.

Dad: "Thank you."

Me: "One more thing I need to tell you."

Dad: "What?"

Me: "As we were driving back to Florida, mom told me something you might enjoy."

Dad: "What's that?"

Me: "She said, since your dad stopped drinking he has turned back into the man I originally fell in love with."

Dad: (in shaky voice) "She really said that?"

Me: "Yes, she really said that."

Dad: "Thanks Kent. That's the best birthday present I've ever received."

Me: "You deserve it."

I didn't know at the time that it would be the last birthday present I'd give to him.

March 2004. My dad was diagnosed with inoperable cancer of the spine and was told he would never walk again and that he had six months to live. My dad was a soldier in the Army. For most soldiers, if a doctor told them that they would never walk again most of them would probably attempt suicide.

Not my dad. He continued to show strength and courage by telling the doctor:

"That's alright, just as long as you prop me up enough so I can see my grandkids."

I would call my dad every single day after that. On Sunday, May 23rd, I called him and promised him I was going to see him in four days and that he and I were going to have a wheelchair race. He said, he's been training for it.

Morning of my flight, I get a call from my brother Vic saying hurry up and get here dad may not make it through the night. I started crying and praying: "Please dad hang on, I'm coming."

I only had one plane ticket. Up until 9/11- 2001, I could fly by myself. Since 9/11 the airlines for the most part required for someone to accompany me in case of emergency. This day, they required my mom to fly with me. I'm so grateful that they did.

We landed in Indianapolis, Indiana at 4:00 p.m. Vic picked us up at the airport and started preparing me for the worst. We got to the nursing home and there were my dad's relatives. Some of whom I had not seen in over twenty years. They attempted to console me and hug me but I just said: "Look, I know you love me, but I'm here for one reason and that's to see my dad. Please let me go see him."

I go to my dad's room. He's on the ventilator, eyes closed, mouth open not moving. My brother puts my dad's hand under my chin so I can hold it. Vic was telling me not to expect much because dad had not shown any sign of movement all day.

I didn't care. I had to tell dad some things before he died. First, I asked my dad did he keep his promise to mom and does he accept the Lord Jesus Christ as his Savior? My dad lifted his thumb and touched me on the cheek. I heard my mom saying: "Thank God." Remember, my brother warned me that dad was not responding to anyone, but he responded to me.

Then I told my dad I knew it wasn't him that was evil. It was the alcohol that made him that way and I told dad that I forgave him for everything that happened.

He moved his two middle fingers in sequential order under my chin to signal "Thank you."

But what convinced me most that he was aware who was talking to him was this. The nurse came in to give my dad medicine. She placed my dad's hand on his bed, pulled me away to give him the medicine. Then she wiped my tears and pushed me back beside him. I forgot to ask her to give me his hand. His hand was on the bed when she left.

I started to tell him that it hurts me to say goodbye but I could not imagine how he was feeling saying goodbye to everyone of us. When I opened my eyes, my dad's hand was holding onto my wheelchair's armrest. I said: "You know who this is don't you? You know it's really me. I love you dad."

That was the last conversation I had with him. Ninety minutes later he passed away with his entire family by his side including the one woman he truly loved, my mom.

I miss him so much. I'm conflicted that I did not want to see him suffer, but at the same time, I felt maybe there were more things to say and to accomplish.

Earlier, I said my dad was a war hero and I told him that on his last birthday in 2003. I did not know until after his death how much of a hero he truly was.

Going through his military records, we discovered that my dad, Master Sergeant Everett M. Bell was awarded on four separate occasions the Bronze Star while in Vietnam. The Bronze Star signifies that a soldier risked his/her life in order to save fellow soldiers. My dad did that four times.

Then, you add the strength and fortitude to stop drinking alcohol cold turkey? Then, after being diagnosed with cancer and being told he could never walk again?

He responds: "That's alright, just as long as you prop me up enough so I can see my grandkids." That is a true hero.

I love you dad, I miss you very much, but I know that you're walking and that you're looking at your kids, grandkids and great-grandchildren and you are grinning from ear to ear and you should stick out your chest with pride. I salute you.

my favorite food is spaghetti

# 3

## My Mom

The term "Momma's boy" usually has a negative connotation. When someone says you're a momma's boy, it usually means you are a weak person who cannot defend or speak up for themselves. In our family if you call my brothers or myself a "Momma's Boy" we will respond with a smile and say thank you. I'm proud to say Yes, I am a momma's boy. If it wasn't for my mom I would either be in a nursing home or I'd be dead.

My mom was born Bobbie Jean Yates on May 22nd 1943 in Bainbridge, Georgia. They did not have ultrasound back then and they thought she was going to be a boy so they picked my grandfather's name Robert Eugene, but when they found out at birth that she was a girl they changed her name to Bobbie Jean.

The family moved back to Lexington, Kentucky a year later. When Grandpa Yates got out of the Army, he couldn't find a job in the south. The north had factories opening and had a lot more jobs available. So, grandma and grandpa moved to Indianapolis, Indiana. Then in 1952 when my mom was nine years old her parents gave her a sister named Willadean.

Mom would never call her sister Willadean because she felt it was unfair she had a boy's name and her sister had a girl's name. So she nicknamed her sister Billie. Years later my aunt Billie legally changed her name to Billie, because she didn't like Willadean either. So, now it is Bobbie and Billie. As my grandma would say, "those are true southern names."

Nine years later in 1961 my mom met a man that would forever change her life.

This is how my mom and dad met in her own words:

"Sonny and I met through my girlfriend Patty Snyder who lived off of 56th street in Lawrence, near the old Lawrence Central High School.

Dad (Sonny) was stationed at Fort Harrison nearby and Patty's brother Tommy worked on cars with dad. (Tommy liked me but I didn't want to go out with him) Patty asked me to go home after school with her and she was going to tell her mom she had to go to the library and used me as an excuse.

Patty wanted to sneak out to meet up with her old boyfriend who looked like "the Fonz", sort of the rebel type and she wanted an excuse to go to the library in Beech Grove, to meet him there and I was the excuse to get out of the house.

Also, dad had gone out with Patty once or twice and she didn't want to date dad, so she used me as an excuse not to go anywhere with him that night.

The first time I saw dad, he was under a car with his legs sticking out. Patty and I wanted to leave, and dad's car was in the way. She told me to go back in the garage and ask him to move his car. He looked out under the car, all greasy and threw me his car keys to me and told me I could move it.

Well, I was so impressed that someone trusted me with his car and let me have the keys. I went out to back it up and it was a new fangled push button car and I couldn't get it in reverse. I didn't know that the gears were push buttons. I was embarrassed and had to go get him and ask him to move it. He was laughing about it.

The next day or later that evening, he asked me out and we just kept seeing each other. He always had a nice car. He had a convertible and took me to the Prom. He didn't drink around me then. My mom and dad didn't want me to date a GI, but I rebelled and did it anyway. I had a curfew to be home by 11 PM, so after he dropped me off at home, he probably went out with his buddies. Anyway, we were inseparable.

Actually, mom was so against it, (we were arguing) and I took mom and dad's car and ran away and drove to Rensselaer one night to see your dad.

The engine in the car blew up, from no oil and poor mom and dad didn't have any money to fix it. Somehow mom and dad came to get me and was dragging me out of Grandma Bell's house in the middle of the night.

My dad had me by one arm yelling and Sonny had me by the other arm pulling me back and yelling "we were going to get married."

The Bells were going to call the police. Finally, mom gave in and left and was crying. I guess all of us kids hurt our parents.

What a night. I guess mom sensed my life was going to be bad. We never listen to our parents do we? I feel really bad now."

## HERE'S MY BIRTH ACCORDING TO MY MOM IN OUR INTERVIEW

<u>Kent:</u> I was born Feb 14th, 1965. When did I appear?

<u>Mom:</u> Before we get into that I remember we lived in a mobile home and I had this urge, (they call it nesting) to clean the house, clean the kitchen cabinets, iron all of my maternity tops, bake a cake and little did I know that I was preparing for your arrival within a few hours because you were not due yet.

The next day was Valentine's Day, so I baked a white cake and placed red cherries on top for Valentine's Day. (P.S. I baked your first birthday cake before you were born. And, no, it wasn't heart shaped like the ones you received for the next 42 years.) I didn't feel good and I had stomach cramps and when your dad got home, (late as usual), we went to bed and I couldn't sleep.

About 3 am I woke up with labor pains and it really wasn't time for you to be born yet. You weren't due for about another month. I wasn't very big in my belly and I always had a "feeling" (premonition) that something was wrong.

<u>Kent:</u> Did I ever kick?

<u>Mom:</u> Well, that was another thing. There was a heartbeat but there wasn't any sonar grams then, (to see the baby before it's born). I could feel you rolling around inside of me, but I didn't think too much about it at the time. I was very busy taking care of two toddlers. Your disability was something I never expected, but I did have feelings that something was wrong.

One time I was having a big argument with your dad because he was a big drinker, going out with his buddies, and I was so frustrated, unhappy, stuck at home with all of the babies and I hated what he was doing to me. So, in a fit of anger when I was yelling at him I said, "I am so sick of you going out and leaving me with a bunch of kids and I just know "something" is going to be wrong and I'll be stuck taking care of a kid with something wrong with it." I don't know why I said it, but little did I know I would be "eating" my words. I just wanted to say something to hurt him for not staying home with me and helping me more.

I really thought the baby might be blind or something. I had a history of having preemies and things never went right, so I had a lot of fears and your dad just didn't seem to care about me at all....

Kent: Now, your in the hospital. They took you to the delivery room. Dad did not go with you? Am I correct?

Mom: No, dad took me, but Vic and Danny couldn't come into the hospital in those days. You had to be 16 years old to go into the hospital or be a patient. They stayed in the car for a few minutes while your dad admitted me. We had no family there to help us and we were new in the neighborhood, so we didn't know anyone yet. We would have never left a child in the car now-a-days, but it was safer back then. Dad couldn't stay with me because he had to go home and take care of Vic and Danny.

In the meantime I was in labor all night and I finally dozed off. When I awoke my doctor was sitting with me and holding my hand. I was in a Military hospital and this was not the normal thing military doctor's did. But, he sensed something was wrong and he knew I didn't have anyone there, so he comforted me.

I want to thank him. I'm not sure of his name, but Dr. Irani's name was on the birth certificate. I'm not sure which doctor actually delivered you, but whatever doctor was on duty and sat with me while I was in labor, I truly want to thank him so much for that and for being supportive. I will never forget it. Then you were born.

Kent: When you had me, when did you think something wasn't right? Was it the look of a nurse or a look of a doctor?

Mom: When I was in the delivery room I kept saying, Oh, I can handle this. I don't need to be put out because they were trying to put a mask on me to put me to sleep. The next thing I know, they put the mask over my face and I was out. When I awoke, I heard a baby crying very weakly.

Because of the weak crying, I felt something was wrong. I saw a black nurse, whose face turned an ashen grayish white color and she had an odd look in her eyes. Nobody was talking and nobody congratulated me nor told me if I had a boy or a girl. Then, a doctor told the nurse to take the bag of afterbirth and the umbilical cord straight to the lab.

Again I knew something was wrong. At first I thought I had another premature baby and that they were going to take you straight to an incubator, (which they did). Before the nurse left the room, I said, "what did I have?" And, she didn't say anything. I asked her again. "what did I have?" Finally, she said a boy. By then they had wrapped you in a swaddling blanket and took you to the baby nursery without showing me. At that time I didn't know about your physical disability, but deep down inside, I knew something was wrong.

They cleaned me up and took me back to my room. They sedated me and I fell asleep. When I woke up Sonny (dad) was standing over me. He looked really shaken. I asked him what's wrong. He said the doctor told me the baby will not live 24 hours and asked where we wanted you buried." Again, I said, "what's wrong?" Your dad said the baby doesn't have any arms or legs.

I said, "oh. your just making that up. Don't say things like that."

He replied, "seriously, he doesn't have any arms or legs and he's going to die."

I said, "Oh, he's not going to die, then I felt like I was fainting.

Since I was sedated, I fell back asleep.

When I came to, I was mad at dad and the doctor's for planning your funeral. I said, "I'm not planning any funeral yet because I didn't want to think about it. I fell back asleep."

When I woke up I was in another room alone. The nurses were taking the other babies down the hall to their mothers for feeding. I sadly looked out the window and was thinking about my baby and I started crying.

I was crying a lot and the nurses never brought me my baby.

I didn't know what to say or what to do. Then a hospital worker stopped by to mop the floor and while he was in the room he tried to encourage me.

He said, Oh, everything's going to be alright. Then a nurse went by and said, John Hopkins University can do miracles. They can do anything for anybody. That was really the only supportive thing that I had at the time.

Later that day, I was really bored and I got up to go down the hall to talk to people because I like to talk to people. I passed a room where a lady had been in the hospital for a few months here. She saw me and motioned me to her bedside. She said, "I need to talk to you." So I went by her bed and sat down in the chair. She said, "I know there is something wrong with your baby."

And I nodded. She said, "I just want to tell you that I have tried to have five children and lost all of them and I decided if I could carry this one to full term, I would take it, no matter what was wrong with it. She was just trying to encourage me.

Well, an army nurse poked her head in the door and said to me sarcastically, "what are you doing in here? She started yelling at me, "You get out of here right now! Your not supposed to be in here."

And I thought, what does she mean? This whole hospital knows about my baby and I was invited into the room. I was really irritated with her attitude.

So I went back to my room and I cried some more. I think some of the rumors around the hospital were people saying I didn't want my baby. I never said that.

And, people gossiped and made stuff up. That really hurt me.

The next day they still hadn't brought my baby to me. So I told the nurse, "I want my baby." The nurses got so excited, but they took me to the nursery because you were in an incubator. They let me see you and hold you and then they started bringing you to me every 4 hours and I started feeding you. That was my hospital experience, but you had to stay for awhile.

Kent: When you did bring me home? Did you and dad have any special plans as to what to tell Vic and Danny?

Mom: Well, we had to call relatives in Indiana, grandma and grandpa and tell them the sad news and we told them you really weren't expected to live more than 24 hours. I remember bringing you home, but I always treated you normal and I just told them, "here's your baby brother." I never made it a point of anything in particular. I just let them see you and we never treated you any different.

Kent: Did somebody come and visit you after the birth? Like government officials?

Mom: Yes. The Food and Drug Administration came to my door and were trying to figure out what caused your birth defects. They asked me if I ever took any drugs? I told them no. I was never a drug user. Then, they asked if I had ever been in Germany or Europe where Thalidomide had been given to pregnant women as a sedative and many children were born like you.

A few years before, hundreds, maybe thousands of children were born in England and Germany and were missing limbs from the drug Thalidomide.

I said, no. But, I do remember getting a hormonal shot to start my monthly cycle when I didn't know I was pregnant. Whatever happened, happened in the first two months of pregnancy.

The Army doctors told me they had given that shot to thousands of women and nothing like this had ever happened. When I went to get a copy of my medical records, the page for that visit had been removed. I still think that may be one of the reasons for your birth defect. With DNA, we might be able to find out now. To this day we do not know why you have these birth defects. We have tried to study it. We have talked to genetic experts and no one has an answer as to why you were born that way.

Kent: When you said the doctor told the nurse to take the afterbirth to the lab for tests and the FDA came to the house, was there anything given to you of any results?

Mom: No. They didn't know anything about DNA at that time. If they knew about DNA, they might have figured out something.

However, the geneticists at Indiana/Purdue University did say-possibly my genes and your dad's genes crossed up. It's an accident of nature and they really do not know. There seems to be no explanation for it.

Kent: You told me while you all lived in Alaska, dad was exposed to Radiation.

Mom: I didn't find that out until about ten years later. Dad was drinking and said something about it and saying, "you can't sue the government while he was in the Military" I was furious that he had kept that secret for so long. And, I blurted out, yes I can sue the government. Then he got quiet and I couldn't get anything out of him.

Later I found out that two other men in his unit had been with him and they had moved a radiation cylinder tube via helicopter or small aircraft. There wasn't much room in the aircraft and he had sat on it. The other men's wives were pregnant at the same time I was.

Mrs. Nosaka had a miscarriage after falling off of a horse, but was told her baby was formed outside the "bag of water." Mrs. Maddox had a baby with some sort of other type of birth defect. We have lost track of these folks over the years and I never could find them to ask questions.

Kent: Now, you have 3 babies under 2 ½ years old. One of them is severely disabled and your husband is a partier. You were basically all alone in Virginia with no family.

Mom: Well, my mom took a month's leave of absence from work and my cousin, Connie came to help me. My mom's sister, Aunt Jenny lived near Virginia in Silver Springs, MD. My mom stayed at Aunt Jenny's. There wasn't much room to stay in our mobile home. For some reason and I don't know why, I just didn't want my mother around. I wanted to do this on my own. I didn't want to burden anyone. I didn't want her to see dad drunk because she was a very religious person and I didn't want her to see that. It was a time of grieving for everyone because all of us were so sad. We didn't know how to act, or interact or talk to each other because we were in shock. There was a lot of thinking to do.

I do remember an insurance man stopping by the house. They used to go door to door to sell things. He saw me crying and I told him what happened and later he sent me big dozen red roses to cheer me up. He was a stranger and I never saw him again. That was the time the song, "Red Roses for A Blue Lady" was popular and every time I hear that song I remember that day. That song means a lot to me.

I had people come into my life at various times that helped me through hardships, but the person I really wanted to help me was your dad and he didn't do much. Either he couldn't handle it so he stayed away and his drinking got the best of him. It was a very difficult time. It was during the Viet Nam conflict and a few weeks later he came home and told me he volunteered to go to Viet Nam. He worked with helicopters in a "critical job" and everyone was going.

That hurt me so much and that's when I started hating him for that and what he was doing to me. He was very Patriotic and I know he wanted to do his duty to his country and I appreciated that he wanted to do that, but at the time I really needed him home.

Someone at his work must have thought that he didn't need to go to Viet Nam and got his orders changed to go to Thailand, (which wasn't any better), but he was gone for 8 months and when he got home, the Army told him he had to go back to the Far East because Thailand didn't count as a combat tour and he would have to do a tour in Viet Nam. Then he had another tour in Viet Nam. So, he served two tours in Nam and one in Thailand. Altogether he served three tours in the Far East.

Kent: At what time was Kim born?

Mom: When dad returned from Thailand about the end of 1965, I got pregnant with Kim and by then the Viet Nam war was turning into a really intense war.

He had to go to Viet Nam this time and by then he didn't want to go back, but he was forced to go. Now-a-days he probably could have received a "hardship" not to go to war, but he didn't get to do that.

We moved to Rensselaer Indiana and lived around his family. Grandma Bell came to stay with us because her husband had died and she needed a place to stay.

Later, when I went to the hospital to have Kim, a dozen roses was delivered to my hospital room from "a secret admirer." Aunt Shirley came in and saw the flowers and I said, "I wonder who they are from." I looked up and a man in a Khaki Army Uniform walked in the door. It was your dad. He looked pretty good then and I was happy for awhile. Then I named my beautiful daughter Kimberly "Rose".

Kent: Now, you have four little children and one of them is disabled. How did you keep your wits?

Mom: I didn't really. After the initial crying about your condition everyday for three years, I finally couldn't cry much. I was really busy with all of the little ones and staying busy is the best way to help depression.

By then I was about 23 years old. I got married when I was

18 and had four children in less than five years. I cried so much. Every time I gave you a bath or when I unwrapped the blanket and saw you I cried for you.

I was probably in a "deep depression" and didn't know it. What helped me, I believe was having the other children and being so busy I didn't have time to feel sorry for myself. By the time I did the laundry, went to the store, cleaned house, went to school activities, church, and all of the things mother's do, I didn't have time to dwell on myself. I did what I had to do.

Kent: You had four small children, a disabled one, and, actually five children counting dad. Your husband is in Viet Nam again and you moved to northern Indiana with your in-laws. Like I said before, how did you keep your wits about you?

Mom: (Laughing) Well, that was an experience. We had our ups and downs and the usual family arguments, but I got through it.

Kent: With so many children to care for, how did you manage to treat us all equally? Did you have a plan as to how to treat each of us? You had so many people to deal with including dad as a fifth child, and you had to divide your attention among so many people, how did you manage?

Mom: Well, I probably didn't balance it out evenly. You took a lot of care. The other kids never complained. They helped do a lot of things for you. They were always around. They brought you toys, propped up your bottle, played games with you like hide and go seek. You could roll around on the floor.

One time we couldn't find you. You had rolled up in a sheet and hid behind the couch. We used to have Easter Egg Hunts in the house so you could roll on the floor and hunt for eggs too. I put the eggs under the sofa, behind the furniture on the floor area, so you could find some too.

Your brothers and sister collected the eggs and put them into a basket for you. They did a lot for you. If they had a piece of candy, they would feed you a piece of candy. It was an automatic thing to do.

They never bathed you or toileted you or anything like that because they were all too little to do that, and I wouldn't have let them.

They were naturally behaved and were very good kids. (That is until they became rebellious teenagers).

Kim became more nurturing for you. She was like a little "mother" to you. You will have to interview her and get her feelings and thoughts about the situation

One time she was waiting outside the house for the "special bus" you were on to go to school and help you when you got off. A much larger boy was making fun of you and as small as she was, she doubled up her fists and knocked him flat on the ground.

I know all of us are more compassionate, unselfish and caring people by having you in our family and living through these experiences.

# 4

## Hi-Jinx Stories

Even though I have no arms or legs I did put my mom through some tough times. I did my share of rebellion and hi-jinx. For instance when we were living in Alaska, I was allowed to attend a regular school. For the first and second grades in Virginia, the schools were not accessible for disabled students so they sent a home tutor for two years. Mrs. Spears was her name and she was and still is a nice lady.

Well, when we moved to Alaska in 1973 you'd think that would be the last place to mainstream disabled students. Nope, in fact, I was the first disabled student to attend regular classes in the district.

The principle brought me into the third grade room and told the teacher Ms. Aunie, "Teach this student."

Well, I was so excited, on attending school that I spent the entire first day in the gym riding around in my electric wheelchair. They called my mom asking where I was because they thought she had picked me up.

She rushed to the school because she thought I went outside of school and didn't know how to get back in. When they found me in the gym, they told me there were certain times to play in the gym and I had to go back to class and learn, which I begrudgingly did.

I had never been to regular school so I didn't know they had rules.

In the summer of 1974, I went to this hospital in Grand Rapids Michigan to get and learn how to use artificial arms and legs. Yes, I used to walk. Well, actually, it was more a waddling motion like a penguin.

I had to stay in the hospital for two months while the prosthesis was being made and for me to be trained. My mom couldn't stay for the two months because of the rest of the family back in Alaska.

So I was there with no family. The staff at the hospital was great because they took in children from all over the world. At that time the Vietnam Conflict was going on and children who were disabled due to land mines or other war injuries would go to this hospital to get new artificial arms or legs.

The first day I had just finished my physical therapy session of walking. The therapist laid me on the mat and placed toys for me to play with while she went to the cafeteria for some coffee. Usually when she goes for coffee she closes a gate so no adult can come in and kidnap any of us.

Well, this day she forgot to close the gate. I've always been a curious child. So when I saw the gate open I thought that I'm going to see what this hospital is really like. So, I roll off the mat and into the hallway for my own personal tour of the hospital. I first roll to the pool. When I say roll, I mean I'm laying on the floor rolling like a log.

After the pool I head towards the cafeteria to check on the therapist. She had just paid for her coffee and was sitting down to drink it. Good, more time to tour. I then headed to the other therapy room because they had the better toys. Hey, I was nine.

After playing in the other therapy room I get on the elevator.

Now nobody is trying to stop me or even paying attention to me. This was a hospital specifically for disabled children so everyone thought I was just getting exercise. I go to my floor, head to my room and fell asleep under the bed. All that rolling can really tire a nine year old out.

All of a sudden I hear on the hospital intercom: "Will Kent Bell please report to physical therapy. Will Kent Bell please report to physical therapy." Then I see the nurses running around looking frantically for me.

I didn't know it at the time but they called my mom in Alaska to ask her if she had taken me home. Her reaction was: WHAT?!!!!!! Now she gets another call saying I'm missing and this time she can't do anything because she's over a 1,000 miles away.

Well, apparently, while I was sleeping a nurse knew where I was hiding because when lunchtime came around she put the tray loudly on the table and said: "Too bad Kent's not here to eat his lunch of cream of mushroom soup over hamburger and raspberry Sherbet for Dessert. Once I heard the dessert, I popped my head out from under the bed and said: "Here I am." I never got in trouble for that stunt but I did scare a lot of people including my mom. Sorry mom.

# 5

# My Brother Vic- The Man of the House

*Danny, Kent, Victor, (front) Kimberly*

This chapter is my interview with my brother Vic.

Question 1. What was your reaction, if any, when you realized I had no arms or legs?

Vic's answer: I was pretty young myself and I do not recall ever thinking that you were different. You were just a baby that needed taken care of like other babies needing fed, diaper changed and all of that jazz. I don't recall ever hearing you cry that much either.

2. Did mom and dad ever sit down with your and talk about my disability?

Vic's answer: This question, as with #1 is based on the premise that I thought you were different. I don't think I ever thought you were different. You just needed help with things.

I do remember getting upset in the middle of the night at times because I envisioned the hardships to come for you and mom would come in and talk to me and calm me down and let me know you would be alright. She was right. That's about the only discussions I remember.

3. What was your reaction when I had to go to the Hospital for days and weeks at a time?

Vic's answer: When you would go to the hospital, the feeling I always had was, I wanted you to be OK. There was always talk by the doctors that you wouldn't live very long and we just wanted you to come back.

There was always the secret hope that you would come back with Bionic limbs (remember, the Six Million Dollar Man was a very popular show at that time.) I could not wait to see you run at super speeds!!

We went to see you on more than one occasion at the hospital and you had made some friends with some of the other patients. How sad I thought it was that some of their families had abandoned them to the hospital and I hoped that maybe we could take a couple of them home with us, so they could have a "normal" family.

It was heartbreaking to see them watch you leave to come home, because I knew they wanted to come too.

I always wondered how family could leave family.

4. Do you remember any funny or crazy stuff we did as kids?

Vic's answer: We were always goofing around. Lots of things come to mind, but I'll keep to a couple of stories that I remember the most of the details.

Generally, you were physically defenseless so I tease you a lot, calling you "loverboy" and you hated that. To my surprise one day, after a good session of "Loverboy", you used your rock heard head and smashed my toes! OUCH!!

Another time I had bugged your room with a wired microphone and I was listening to and recording you. When my equipment stopped working, I went to investigate and found that you had smashed a steel microphone to pieces with your hard head!! You found it!!

Another time you and I were being babysat by one of our cousins. He was teasing you unmercifully and to the point that I picked you up and was going to carry you to Grandma Bell's trailer a couple of miles away. I was a little bitty thing myself.

I had you on my shoulder and as I ran towards the front screen door, I went to push it open with my left hand and the door didn't open. I just put my hand through the upper screen and the center support acted as a bar that flipped us through the upper opening and we both hit the concrete, head first!

I don't remember the medical treatment. (Maybe cousin Debbie fixed us up since she was a nurse practitioner.)

I could go on and on with stories, but I'll close this question with the scariest story in my mind.

Paul's Trailer Park in Rensselaer Indiana had cornfields on three sides and a huge cemetery to the south across the street, (always the formula for a nightmare.)

It seemed like the drinking water and the bath water came straight from the Iroquois River. It was "sulfur water" and really smelled.

You had to pinch your nose so you couldn't smell the water if you were going to drink it, (which we never did.) We use to go into town to Aunt Shirley's and fill up jugs of drinking water because she had city water and that water tasted better.

When we spent the night there, all of us kids slept on the floor in the living room. This was not out of the ordinary. It was a two bedroom trailer and Grandma had her room, mom and dad had the guest room and all of us slept in the living room on the floor in front of a fan.

The fan we used on this night was a tube that blew the air down and out in all directions and we were all spread out in front of it like the spokes on a wheel.

As the night progressed, the storms got worse. Lighting flashed and thunder crashed. Tree branches were moving up and down and side to side outside the main bay window and at times they were scratching the glass.

They looked like huge skeletal hands from the graveyard across the street.

Shadowed by the lightning flashed was a chair and to me it looked like a headless man was sitting there. I turned and saw you. I saw a white trail flowing from the top of your head, just like some of the ghosts from the Casper the friendly ghost cartoons.

You weren't moving, but the trail was gracefully flowing. You were a GHOST!

I was horrified! I could not move, and I could not scream or utter a sound. I expected at any moment you would levitate into the air, open your eyes and bare your fangs, bite me and take me into eternity with you!

Somehow "DAD" came out of my mouth and when dad turned on the light, your ghostly trail was just a white T-shirt you had almost rolled out of, the neck of the shirt was positioned like a headband and the rest was blowing the breeze from the fan above your head. The headless man in the chair was just a long jacket hanging over the back of the chair!

Boy, was I glad when that light came on!!

My last question to you: What have I taught you if anything?

Vic's answer: This question is an easy and short answer. No matter how tough things are, work, relationships, finances etc; you have it harder than I do.

If you can deal with your hardships, I can deal with anything that comes my way.

I will always try to be there to help when you need it brother…

YOU ARE MY HERO…

I LOVE YOU…VIC

# 6

# Daniel My Brother

*Kent and Danny and the Plaid Pants*

Well, Kent, here is my story about you. This is a tall order. But actually, it is a lot simpler than you might think. You see, when you were born, I was all of only 16 months old, younger than my own son Jack is right now.

There was no 'reaction' for me. I guess a baby is a baby, and anything different about you wasn't really apparent to me as an issue.

I'm sure that I must have thought at some point about the fact that you didn't have arms or legs, but only Mom would be able to say whether I asked about that specifically.

Growing up with you as a family member makes perfect sense, and I don't think I ever thought that anything was weird or different.

Thinking about it now, I guess I would have viewed everyone else's family as 'different', because they had nobody like you in their lives. For example, the childhood friends I had, I didn't see anything interesting about their siblings at all. I guess I must have thought that their lives were pretty dull.

My friends were always interested in my little brother, but I wasn't ever interested in their siblings.

Life with you always presented some fun and interesting opportunities. I mean, I didn't know anyone that had a wheelchair that they could fool around with, or be amazed by any of the interesting and wonderful gadgets that were a part of your accouterments.

And what's more, I don't think it seemed to me that anybody I knew were as close to any of their siblings, that they must have lacked a bond that I felt among us.

Because of your condition, I think that I remember that we all had very imaginative ways of playing which would include you, and these involved tumbling about and roughhousing in football type games on the floor with you.

That all resulted in a lot of physical contact, which I think in turn had always built up a stronger bond. To be able to get you to go up or down the stairs, that was a lot of fun, just the simple things that kids do together.

I think, though, that we may have played games that involved protecting you in some way, like cops and robbers, and you may have been a person to be guarded, protected, in some way.

But I also remember wanting to have you on my side, because you had some special abilities in other ways, in our games. Maybe like a superhero, I must have imagined that, since you couldn't walk, you could fly, or float.

You could break down barriers built with pillows in a way that I never could, in an exciting way, like a bulldozer, a powerhouse, and in the sports type games, you were a blocker, and a line-breaker. You are always a real pal, a buddy, and a true friend.

I am sure that many of these other people must have shared similar bonds among their siblings. But I think the weird thing was when a 'sister' (ugghh) came along. Now you know I love our sister with all of my heart, but for little boys, of course that sister was the one who didn't fit in.

She probably had a tough time of it for awhile I am sure. I remember teasing her, excluding her, just the normal things that boys might do. But I think we were really protective of you.

I think that I was confused if outsiders asked me how I felt about your condition. I must have wondered what the heck they were talking about.

That would have been like saying something like, 'why does your sister have blonde hair, and how do you deal with that?' or, why does your dad's feet smell when he takes off his boots?

Why do ya'll have a pet cat? Why do you wear glasses? It is how it always was, I don't think I ever thought that I was different, it was that they were the strange ones, with strange families, somehow incomplete, or lacking in something special that we all shared.

I think I must have perceived that, despite the conflict that raged between mom and dad, we were a very loving and tightly knit family bound together in love.

I would not be much help to try and describe any anguish or conflicted feelings. As a child, none with regard to you. We had a strong Christian background and church participation. I remember we used to jockey for the privilege of pushing your wheelchair!

The only anguish and conflict I ever felt has been as an adult, wishing that I could have been more a part of your life, to help care for you in more ways, to relieve the stress that Mom and others may have felt, to sort of have done more of what I had perceived as my fair share.

Maybe from the sidelines, I like to think that I suggested the whole VA thing, and that in a roundabout way I had helped to ensure at least a minimal provision for you.

I like to think that you are ok, at least on a minimal level, and am always pleased to know of your experiences and accomplishments, and thank God that you have been able to have so much meaning and multiple facets to your life.

I still encourage you to diet drastically, as we both could stand to lose a few pounds.

So that leads to the second question, and I don't simply have recollection of any necessity by our parents to explain anything, because it was not anything that ever needed to be explained.

I must assume, though, that I must have at some point asked why, and I would only be guessing about a response that would have included something like, that is the way God made Kent, or that nobody (like the doctors) knows why, it just happened.

You see, that is the wonderful thing about children and about being a child. A child is full of love and kindness, understanding and acceptance. They only learn how to be negative, mean, and spiteful as they grow up, and get an onslaught of adult feelings and issues thrown at them.

The beautiful fact of a child's innocence lets me know that God has made man to have an inherently good, kind, and loving nature. At least that is what I get from that.

Ignorance, and fear, is the root of all evil. When a child is loved unconditionally, that child grows to be a true human being.

Hospitals. I remember you going to hospitals, but I never associated that with any danger as a child.

The only time I remember worrying was later, when, as an adult, I found out only afterwards that, while I was in the Army, you were in the hospital for a time and that you had been very ill, but Mom never told me because she didn't want me to worry. And I was angry at her for that, though I know it was motivated out of her love for me.

But I would have wanted to get there, to be with you, and to let you know how much I have loved you and have loved having you as a part of my life, were you to be called away.

Had I missed that opportunity, I guess I would be fairly bitter to have not been informed. The childhood incidents never caused me concern, because I must have known that you would be ok.

I never as a child worried about you passing away, and if I did, with such a strong Christian life, I was sure that you would go to heaven. But later, as an adult, I have had much more worry and anguish about that subject, and have shed tears on my own to contemplate the day that your light may be extinguished (if that comes before me).

Funny and crazy? Well I remember being a child with you was always fun, in whatever we did. I think your own crazy antics are more of your story, because I don't remember daring to do anything 'crazy' anyway.

Just being a regular kid, with mostly regular kid games, that's how I remember it.

You have taught me that life is a wonderful gift, on any level, and that life is precious for every living thing. But then there are times that I cannot apply these things to my own life, in ways that are hard to describe.

To take pleasure in and enjoy the simplest of the things that life has to offer. To praise God at the glory of His work, this world, and the life that we have.

The sunrise, nature, the taste of a pineapple, a hug, the warmth of a good coat, the sound of the crickets and the smell of the ocean. And an ice-cold coke.

Everything else we have is just an illusion, a distraction, and a consequence of circumstance, mostly. I mean like, money, house, car, etc.

So many variety of things line up in different ways for different people, and while one can act in ways to get in a certain direction, and certainly achieve goals in that regard, those material goals are the illusion.

The true measure is something you can't touch, but certainly can feel. Knowing you has taught me to love in a true sense, the life that I have, for all of its ups and downs, gains and losses, victories and defeats.

I struggle to prove worthy of the blessings in my life, and though I am burdened, and weary, I soldier on through a forest of adversity, to try to remember to enjoy the respite of the meadows along the way, and try not worry so much about where the journey is leading.

# 7

## Kent's Thoughts.....

In regards to Daniel thinking about me as a superhero, and creating ways to have fun, I remember one of many instances. We were in Rensselaer visiting Grandma Bell. He took me swimming. He took me under his arm and we went underwater like a submarine and he used me as a missile. Fun times.

Amongst the children, Daniel was the only other sibling who was kind of into sports. He played Pop Warner Football in Alaska. The team he was on was called the Bengals. He played Defense. The team went all the way to the State Championship and won the SNOW BOWL title.

There was only one time when I went to the same school as my brothers. When I was in 5$^{th}$ grade, my brother Vic was an 8$^{th}$ grader and my brother Daniel was a 7$^{th}$ grader. Both of my brothers are book smart. Wait, they're book geniuses.

When I finally reached the 7$^{th}$ grade the teachers in the Junior High grades was excited to have another Bell to teach.

Unfortunately, my smarts was and still is street smarts and smart aleck. One of my teachers, Mr. Romeo asked me why I couldn't be more like my brothers Vic and Danny who constantly got A'S on all their tests. I replied because I'm not Vic or Danny, I'm Kent.

So to those who have intelligent older siblings, and the

teacher asks you why can't you be like your older brother/sister? Just say, I'm not them. I am my own person.

I don't have children of my own because I've never been married. But thanks to my brother Daniel my name does live on. When his first son Mitchell was born.

Daniel and Mitchell's mother, Stacy decided the child's name would be Mitchell Kenton Bell. That's right, I have a kid named after me. I asked Daniel why he did that? Here is his response:

"I admire your strength and courage. You are my role model and hero for what you have accomplished. I want my son to have the same strength and courage as you have." To this day, that is the best words someone has ever said to me and putting my name into your son is the greatest honor bestowed to me. Every time I see or talk to him I know that he will always be a part of me. Thank you.

*Danny, Victor, Kimberly, Kent*

my favorite color is green

# PHOTO GALLERY

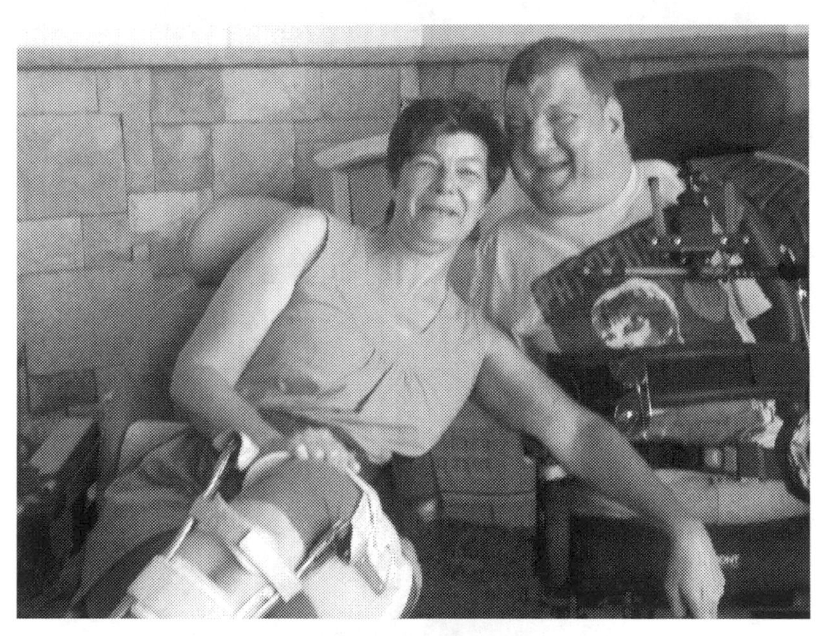

*Cindy Jameson and Kent*

*Kent Waterskiing-UCANSKI2*

*Kent with Emmy Award*

*Kent at Soccer*

*Kent Typing*

*Kent and USA Olympics Basketball Player Tim Duncan*

*Kent's Sister Kim on Cruise*

*Mom, Kent, Kim*

*Kent's Book on Fox News*

*Lance Hunt, Jim Klein, Joe Folsom, Toni Bush Holes and Kent*

*Lifelong Best Friends, Jason, Curtis and Kent*

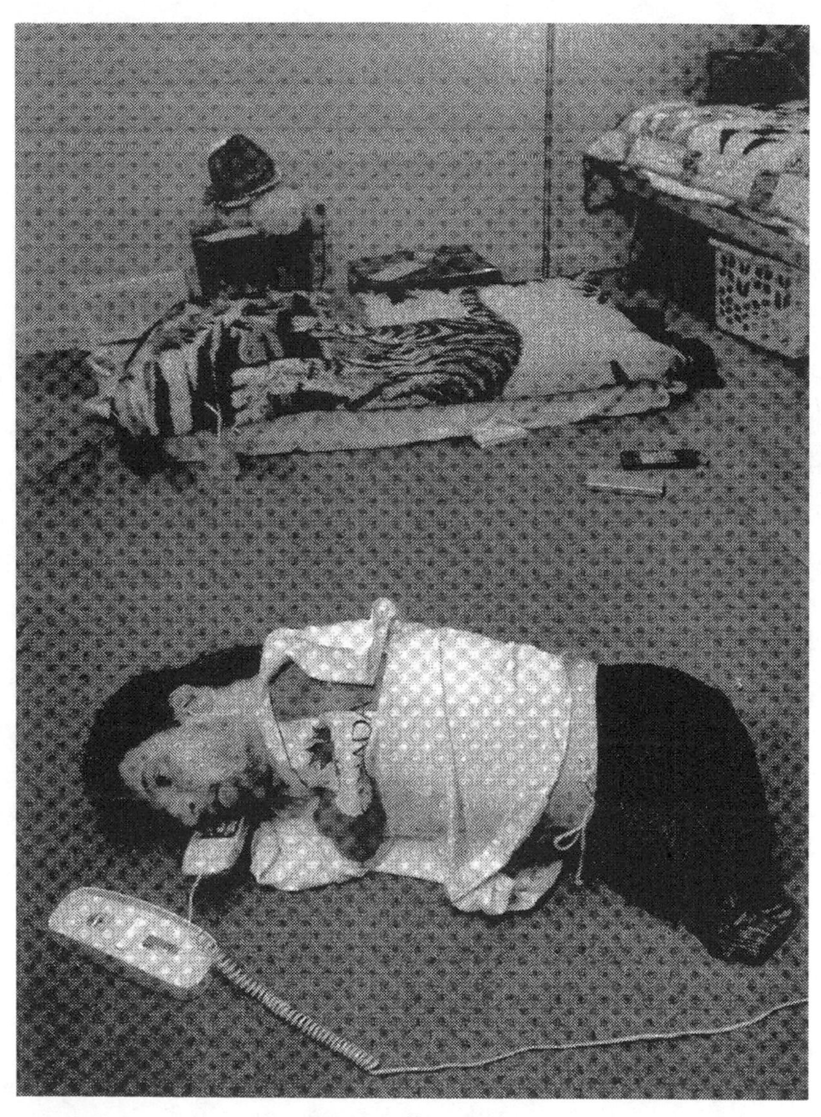

*Kents College Dorm*

*Shannon and Mary*

*Michele, Joey, Isiah, Luke*

*Dad's Sisters and Brother, Aunt Shirley, Uncle Dick, Aunt Barb*

*Kent Soccer Tournament*

*Kent with Emmy Award*
*Best News Story of the Year*
*Fox News Jacksonville, FL*

*Dad, Christopher, Santa, Jennifer, Kent*

*Dad and Mom, Military Retirement Ft. Harrision, IN, US Army*

*Brother Dan, Military*

*Kent, Future Graduate*

*Kent*

*Kent, Neice, Great-nephew*

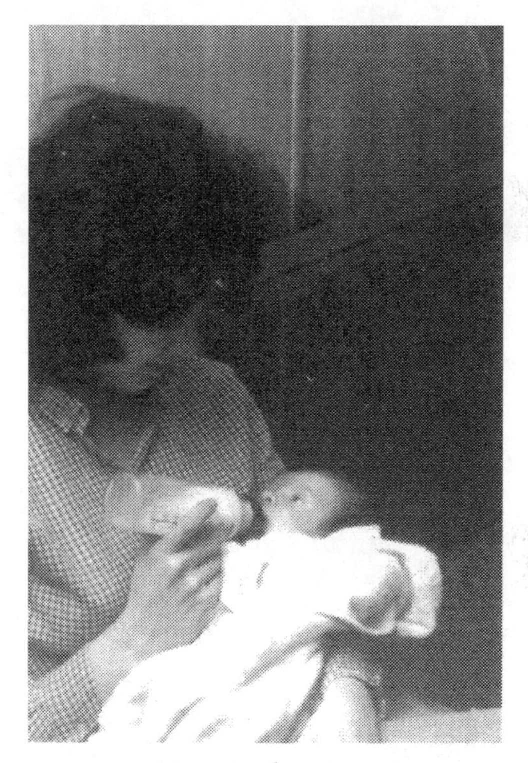

*Mom Feeding Kent*

*Mom, Cindy, Kent*

*Playing in Snow with Brothers and Sister, Alaska*

*Erin and Kent*

*Kent at Score Table, University of North Florida*

*John Chestnut, My Wonderful Stepdad*

*Aunt Billie*

# 8

# Kim's Story

*Kim and Kent*

## WHEN I REALIZED KENT HAD NO LIMBS. . .

I don't remember any significant moment. I've always known and never questioned it. I suppose I just realized that God made you that way. Mom tells me that I never asked her. You were my older brother, my pal.

I automatically did things for you. I walked around with

a bottle and would stick it in your mouth and bring mom whatever she needed for you.

I was a low maintenance child myself because mom was very busy. She told me I used to bring her a clean diaper and told her I needed changed. I suppose I did the same for you. Whatever I needed I assumed you needed too.

We were only one year, six months and one day apart. I was closer to you than anyone else. (I still am most of the time.) I used to think it was me and you and then there was them. We shared a room in our younger days and remember playing together and giggling a lot before we went to sleep. I was fortunate to learn things early. You were home schooled so that meant I was too for awhile. But, the teacher Mrs. Spears (I still remember her), let me sit in the first half until lunch. By then we were giddy and I had to go away so you could actually learn. We laughed too much and couldn't concentrate.

## A VERY VIVID MEMORY I HAVE. . .

I was in kindergarten so I had half days of school. We shared a bedroom in Virginia. I had a twin bed and you slept in a crib. I was always under the impression that you could go to the hospital and never come home.

I guess the doctors always told mom you wouldn't live another year, so I knew your health was an issue. Anyway we had always shared a room and one day, I came home from school and ran up to the room to greet you so we could play and you weren't there. Your bed and toys were gone.

I remember standing in the bedroom doorway, stunned.... My first reaction was tears. I thought out of the blue you had died while I was at school. You were just gone. It had happened, the Lord called you home. It never dawned on me that mom and dad had moved you into the bedroom with our brothers. I was too young to know that it was time that we had to be separated.

Some nosey neighbor thought it was her business to make an issue out of the fact that a boy and girl shared the same room. (special circumstances).

Although we were still very young, we had only a three bedroom apartment. So Kent, Vic and Dan had to be cramped up in a room and I ended up with my own room.

I think you guys resented me for that. It wasn't my doing though. But, for a very long time I cried all night. I didn't want my own room and I missed you. I had to have the lights on at night for what seemed like an eternity. I was scared.

I ran around looking for you and mom explained the boys had to be in one room. It was the law. I was greatly relieved to know that you were okay and still my brother.

Time to grow up huh…I didn't understand. I thought I did something bad and I was being punished. I wasn't allowed to share a room with you anymore. What had I done wrong?

It had always been them and us. Now it was you guys and me. Separate

## TRICK OR TREATING

Another story I remember is Halloween. One year we were visiting Grandma and Grandpa Yates. Grandma would have a cookout for all the neighborhood kids when we were there. She loved to celebrate anytime she saw her grandchildren.

Anyway, every year no matter what, I would take two trick or treat bags. One for you and one for me. Mom would push your wheelchair while I would knock on doors. Vic and

Dan were way ahead of us. Most places had steps and weren't accessible for you, so you would be at the end of the steps. In costume of course, I never thought much of it until some lady in grandma's neighborhood yelled at me for having two bags. I explained one was for my brother in a wheelchair and we can't get him on your porch. She didn't believe me. There were lots of kids around. It was very crowded and she wasn't nice and told me I got no candy because I was greedy. I waited until everyone left and then pointed out toward the street. There you were with mom waiting at the end of the sidewalk. She looked and said, Oh! gave me a piece of candy for each bag. She should have been embarressed.

Don't know if she was or not, but she sure was stingy with the candy. She never even apologized to me. I was hurt.

It never occurred to me to take advantage. I was just doing what I always did. Do for my brother what he can't do for himself.

More of Kims Story:

## BRUSH WITH DEATH:

Many tears and loads of laughter are what come to mind. Memories…there are just too many to put on paper. I suppose the diagnosis of kidney failure is the one that is at the forefront of my mind. The events that took place three years ago were life changing again.

Kent, you had coughed for many months and you had thought that it was a symptom from allergies. My persistence in getting you to a doctor was annoying to you, I know. But, I knew in my gut that something else was going on. Making arrangements sounds simple to others, but we know the complexity of just getting you to the doctor. You were referred to a Respiratory Specialist who decided you needed blood work. Terrifying!! Not a simple test for you. I remember trying to make an appointment and the receptionist had a difficult time comprehending that your blood work has to be drawn in a hospital and not a doctor's office and is an actual medical procedure. Your blood has to be drawn from your neck vein.

In the meantime we missed our bus and had to wait three more hours for another one.

Things were stressful and scary. Discussing having blood work, mom explained that you didn't have to go through with it due to the risk. Prior years this procedure was very complicated. The procedure has come a long way. For you, they said it was simple to run a pick line into your neck. An appointment was made for the following Monday. We knew we were in for a long day, but the events that followed will forever sadden me.

Hospitals always have an issue about having someone to transfer you from your chair to a hospital bed. It usually ends up being mom or I because they just can't figure it out. It's so simple but others over think things. Finally, you are in the bed and hours go by. No one wants to take responsibility of trying to put a needle in your neck. They are scared. When people see you they are shocked. The medical profession should be used to it because of all the wounded warriors coming home.

Again, hours later a doctor came in and placed a pick line in your neck in a matter of minutes and I was furious that a whole team of people couldn't or wouldn't do it. He was a doctor from the emergency room and we had to wait until he had a free moment.

"Almost painless," you said, Although, it looked painful to me. They drew some blood. I don't remember how long it took to get the results. But, the next thing we knew, the doctors cancelled the cat scan. The results were devastating. Your kretin levels were so high they couldn't risk putting dye in you for a cat scan. They had you in a room without us and sent you for an x-ray of your kidneys. They left us in the dark and just blurted out to you without telling the family to help you through the horrible news that that you needed a kidney transplant and that you were in stage 5 kidney failure. No bed side manner at all. Just left you there by yourself while we were in the waiting room wondering what in the world was going on. Finally, they allowed us to see you, one at a time. I remember tears rolling down your face, no hands to wipe them away. I said, "oh, my God Kent. What's wrong? You said, "I need a kidney transplant and instant shock took over. What the HELL? We were told you would have probably died in a week or so from a massive heart attack.

A doctor came by to try to comfort you for minute. He said, "no worries." He is 100% sure you will have a transplant in about three months and be back to normal. It's alright. Wait here for your mom. This was the beginning of another huge disappointment. During these discussions, they didn't seem to think your mom would need an explanation. I jumped up and said he can have my kidney now. Then I remembered I can't donate any organs due to my blood disorder. I found it doesn't work like that. I went and got mom and I was distraught. The look on my face was indescribable. She said, "what's wrong?" I sent her into the room next.

That's when we found out about the HIPAA LAW. What a bunch of crap! The staff treated mom terribly. "For your protection" they said, Protection from what? Protection from whom? They acted as if your family really had nothing to do with it and they were taking over. That was it! No consultation, no second opinion, no nothing. We were speechless, but only for a moment.

You were getting admitted to the hospital, and we were left in the dark. We tried to be with you to comfort you. The hospital didn't make it easy for sure. Everyone in the family was crying.

We sat in the Emergency Room and fifteen hours later, about nine o'clock at night before we got you checked into the hospital. We were unfamiliar with the hospital and we didn't know where to go, had to walk for miles from the parking garage. We had walked and walked until we were exhausted.

When they finally got you into a room, there was no privacy and we were trying to figure out what was next. You were so scared and alone, even with people around you. Cindy, your girlfriend wanted some time with you, and she said we looked worn out and needed some rest. So mom and I decided to go home and get some things because we lived across that state line in Georgia, a long way from the hospital. We had already been at the hospital all night, and we knew we would be at the hospital for many days to come, maybe weeks.

Later that morning Cindy called us frantic saying, "they are taking him away Kim, to do a procedure called dialysis!" There wasn't any discussion with mom or family about dialysis, nor what was going to come about. Cindy said, "I begged them to wait until you got back and told them you were on the way, but they were so rude and said you have no choice." They told you that you would die now if you didn't have this procedure done! You had no choice, and you were dumbfounded.

Cindy continued to say, "Kent and I are begging them to wait on his family. They don't care." He doesn't know what's going on."

Boy, I have never seen my mom so mad in my life. They only came in when we weren't there. It seemed like it was almost on purpose. We rushed back and were asking questions and nobody would give us a straight answer. They were avoiding us.

The HIPAA law prevented them from letting us know what was going on. You are an adult, that's it. You are an unmarried adult, so I thought they would tell mom about you. It is not the case. What really irked mom and I was that one of the staff started to tell Cindy, who wasn't even a relative, details about your condition, yet treated mom like it was none of her business.

Obviously you have no say so about your own medical treatment. No one even discussed and explained what dialysis is all about. Kent, "you said the worst part of this disaster is that you feel you have NO CONTROL OVER YOUR OWN LIFE." How terrifying. What a nightmare! We were all stepping into the twilight zone.

They finally let us into the dialysis room and they were very stand offish. Finally, on the third day they suggested we talk to a social worker. She informed mom that she could get a medical power of attorney, (which made things chaotic, because it was impossible to run out and get one as we were at the hospital 24 hours a day.). They didn't have anyone in administration available to do this for us. They could only notarize things.

They couldn't get it through their thick heads that you wanted and needed your family to be involved. Who do they think they are? Example: If you were an unmarried adult and in a car accident the people in the hospital would contact the parents and would surely tell them the details.

The whole thing was ugly and prevented us from simply being by your side to help you process this horrible situation and to be a comfort to you. That's all we wanted, To be there for you. You are so loved and if I could have taken it away, I would have. I prayed really hard about that, for God to bring you out of this pain and deliver you, to give you strength and comfort. Make you VICTORIOUS! And, really you are VICTORIOUS!. You are the bravest human being I have ever known! My admiration for you is above all.......

Now, for the really ugly stuff. They stuck a needle into your neck. They ran a catheter out of your neck for dialysis and basically, you couldn't move. I think they had gone too far up into your neck. You got through your first dialysis treatment and needed rest, so we sat in a chair and stood. There was nowhere to sit. We were not leaving you alone for a moment. We were always by your side. I couldn't fathom how I was going to lift you with this catheter protruding out of your neck and chest. I thought one wrong move and I could kill you.

I came to sit with you during the second or third treatment. The hospital did allow that. As soon, as I walked up to you and said "hello" I saw your eyes roll back and you were gone. I started yelling for help, grabbed your stick out of your mouth and a nurse came over calmly and said she would handle it. Apparently they flip the bed at an angle to get the blood back to your head. This would be a common occurence for you due to the fact that your blood pressure cannot be monitored during treatments, which is vital!

I got out of the way and ran to the chapel, two doors down from dialysis. I dropped to my knees at the alter crying, my entire body was shaking uncontrollably. I begged for God to spare you. I called mom hysterical crying and saying I saw him die, Mom, I saw him die! His little body can't take it. Mom said, "I'm on my way. Try to stop crying Kim. Please." Keeping mom on the phone, it took a few moments, but I finally came back into the room. And there you were, ALIVE!

You told me you don't remember any of this incident. Incredible!

It didn't take long and the nurses were talking about your release. Doctors didn't have much contact with mom to explain things. We stayed in the room constantly waiting to talk to doctors. One might stop by occasionally, but had no real answers. It was this doctor, then another doctor, all asking the same questions over and over again. Occasionally if one of us had get a snack or go to the bathroom, it seemed it was during that time a doctor had stopped by and we didn't have a chance to ask our questions. Mom had always been the one to communicate with the doctors and you didn't know a lot of the answers. None of us were familiar with what dialysis was and there was nobody to council us. The third day the nephrologist came by and he answered questions and some pieces of the puzzle were coming together. All of our lives were changed forever.

A few days later, right before your release a physician's assistant (PA), Roy F. from the dialysis center came on his own time when he heard about you and that you would be a patient at the clinic where he worked. He didn't present himself as a doctor but we looked upon him as if he was an MD, because he so informed and was the only person who took the time to try to understand your situation. He explained to us that the catheter is a temporary solution to give you dialysis and that he believed that you could have what is called a (graft) surgically implanted in your chest across from your heart in the shape of a loop to receive dialysis. All patients have a fistula implanted in their arms or legs to receive dialysis. Of course, you don't have those options. Roy was a God send. Our heads were spinning with questions. What a welcome relief that someone had talked to us! Thank God for him! We learned more in one hour from him than we had learned from anyone in days at the hospital. You agreed to the surgery and a heart surgeon would do the surgery before you left the hospital. But, this was not the end of this nightmare for you.

I don't remember how long it was until your surgery, but aftercare was a whole other undertaking. The medical staff acted as if it was no big deal. Your life won't change much. Just throw in dialysis three days a week and life goes on as normal. Dialysis consumes your life. All the questions as to how all of this goes down. There were no real consultations of any kind.

Surgery went as good as can be expected, but not as simple as people might think. There is no real way to check your blood pressure while under anesthesia. At least there used to not be a way. The professionals said they would use what is called an A-line to check it while you were under. It was always risky. Many times during the next three years, a needle was stuck in your neck near your vein to give you antibiotics when you contracted a deadly infection called ORSA/MRSE and had other illnesses. Mom was told if there was one mistake inserting the needle, it could kill you.

By late evening they brought you to your room and acted like your recovery was "no big deal." It was a huge deal!

Mom was exhausted. I thought she was going to collapse. So, I told the nurses I don't know their policy, but I was staying in that room with you overnight, (even if I had to go to jail over it!) What if something happened to you and you needed assistance. You can't use a call button and the nursing staff was short handed.

One nurse had the nerve to tell me that the patient next to you could call for help for you. Oh, my God I thought! They have to be kidding! What were they thinking! This man next to you is half dead himself and sedated. What kind of operation is this hospital running here? My brother is of special needs and obviously they are not equipped to handle the situation at hand. They had no answer and I just stayed and told mom to go home for awhile and I would not leave your side.

It wasn't long and you began to vomit. And I tried to lift you forward so you wouldn't choke to death. I began frantically hitting the nurses call button and trying to use two hands to hold you up while you were vomiting all over. I thought you were going to die right then and there. You needed constant assistance and monitoring.

It took too long for someone to come and help. A nurse, I hadn't seen before finally made it to me because everyone was busy with other patients. She was already off of work and stepped up to the plate in a time of crisis. This was a true crisis. I truly believe if I had not been there, you would have died. After everything you had endured in that week, simply choking on your own vomit because you cannot roll over or sit yourself up.

I was scared and furious at the same time. Needless to say, I think you thought this was the end. This went on for awhile and I was terrified for you. After about an hour they finally accepted the fact they didn't have the skills or manpower to care for you and made a decision to move you to the heart wing of the hospital where you could get your own room and more skilled care. No sh## Sherlock. That's what I have said all along. One nurse rose to the call, (over and above her duty) and stayed after her shift for hours to personally transport you to the heart wing. I could see her face and she just wanted to cry, but didn't.

She knew you needed to be in another wing, but she had no say so in the decision. She was the best nurse in the whole place.

Thank you Ginger M. You were another "God Send." You are what a nurse is supposed to be. We thanked her constantly and you called her an "Angel". And she was!

Finally you were moved to the other wing of the hospital. We finally had some relief. I sat in a chair all night to make sure you were breathing. The next day mom and I were all there with you and officials were talking about sending you home again. I couldn't believe it. There was NO WAY you could be home alone at any point. I told them I need time to prepare your apartment for your new needs. In the meantime, mom was trying to get you into a Rehab facility so you could have 24 hour nursing care. We were told that the only place at that time who had dialysis was Brooks Rehab, but since you could not exercise or what they considered Rehab, they were not going to send you there. No matter what mom said, nobody would listen. They wouldn't even listen to you. They didn't even suggest another place for nursing care. We thought they sent you home to die.

You would have to have a gurney brought in three times a week to be taken to dialysis and arrangements needed to be made. I had to get rid of furniture and sterilize your apartment. It is quite small. People don't realize you roll on the floor to get around and everything is on the floor for you. This would be a time consuming task. The next day I spent all day cleaning, sterilizing and I remember we had to bring a truck and trailer from Georgia to move things. Mom, John and I had so much to do before you came home. We begged the hospital to briefly have you in a rehab center and they said no. They said they could not "justify" it on the paperwork. You had surgery, a catheter sticking out of your chest and could not roll over at all. You needed 24 hour care. So, mom and I took turns with you 24 hours a day. We tagged team every three days. We got up at 5am every other day and prepared you for dialysis and rode transport and stayed in the lobby until your session was finished and rode transport home with you. Dialysis would not let us go in the back to be with you. It just isn't their policy. It's frustrating because, later, we learned people with cancer can have a family member sit with them during the cancer treatments.

Let me go back to the transport problems. Transport said to be ready at six am and most times, we didn't get home until two or three pm. Your dialysis is 3½ hours long, but the rest of the time is waiting for transport. You were so scared every day. We never left you alone through this terrible experience in your life. In time you have settled in to the routine and your attendant takes care of a lot of things for you.

In closing I want to say this: There are many siblings of a child with disabilities across the world and I would hope all of them feel the same as I do.

Some may have resentment for the attention that it takes to care for the child that can't care for themselves. Not me. Mom has always needed me, so I apologize to the both of you for not always being there during my teenage years in your many times of need.

Facing life everyday in your condition is an act of bravery, but to face death everyday is beyond imaginable and exceeds bravery. You do this every day! Most would give up, but not you. No one has more of a will to live than you. All of your suffering makes you want to do more. Be more. God must have big rewards for you someday Kent!

It's a great humbling experience for the rest of us.

I look at it this way. God made me your sister for a reason and I am by brother's keeper. You're my brother and I love you. I am here now and have been for a number of years and wouldn't trade it for anything Kent. You are never alone.

NOTE: At the time of this printing, Kent has been on dialysis five years. Mayo Clinic and Shands at Gainesville denied you a kidney transplant even with seven people offering you their kidney.

# 9

# Grandma's Story

*Grandpa, Grandma, Aunt Billie and Mom*

It was over 35 years ago. I shall never forget the morning when I walked into my place of work. I never expected to hear the news that I received that my grandson was born without limbs. The shock was overwhelming to me.

I sat my supervisor's desk and had a good cry. He tried to comfort me by telling me that he had a cousin who had a child that was born without limbs. A child that he had never seen, but the fact remained that he too had heard about her, made me feel that he understood our sadness.

I was in no mood to do a good days work and he suggested that I take a month's leave of absence to go and be with my daughter and son-in-law, Bobbie and Everett Bell, who was living in Virginia, where Kenton was born.

Being a Christian and having witnessed for my Lord, I hoped I had helped many people with my Christian living. I have always loved people and tried so hard to help people whenever they had a problem. I accepted the leave of absence from my job. I went home bewildered and concerned as how my daughter and son-in-law were doing.

I have been a person of prayer and faith in God, but this time, I had many mixed emotions. As I went to my prayer room and began to pray, All I could do was cry and sob. My thoughts were, Why, Why, Why?

After all, I had lived for the Lord and I had brought my children up to serve and to believe in Jesus Christ the Savior of the world. How long I was on my knees I can't say. It seemed like it was hours.

I knew in my heart that God was my answer and after some time that seemed like a century, I finally said to the Lord, "I know that you have a reason for all of this.. Please forgive me for doubting you."

The Lord immediately began to talk to me and I calmed myself to listen to him. He drew my attention to the fact that many a time I had prayed that he would save my children. The lord seemed to impress me to turn loose of the situation and let Him have it. I did. I finally said, "Not our will, Lord, but yours be done." I felt God's presence and He assured me that

He was in control and lifted the burden off me. God never leaves us nor forsakes us. I thank Him for this.

The Hymn comes to my mind and I quote, "Does Jesus care when my heart is grieved? Oh, yes, He cares, I know He cares. His heart is touched with my grief. When the days are dreary and my heart grows weary, I know HE cares for me."

Needless to say, I had even prayed that God would take Kenton home with Him, even though, this too, would have been hard to accept.

As time goes on I continue to pray for all of my grandchildren and my two daughter's Bobbie and Billie.

My husband was a Christian also and he was struggling with his own emotions. Such as it was with all of us.

God has been a great comforter for us and Kenton and my grandchildren are the greatest!!!

They all have been such a blessing in so many ways and I know God has used them many times. When perhaps they themselves were unaware of it, I had the privilege of having them for 2 years when their father was in Viet Nam fighting for our country.

They have great potential of becoming anything they want to accomplish. I love each of them. We make no differences in our concern for each of them. Each one is unique in their own right. This I love and respect.

When they were young we kept them in church and had them in plays, and Bobbie, my daughter did everything she could to develop their talents and to give them good instruction.

Just like most teenagers, they haven't always accepted this, but like all of the rest of us all growing up our hope is, if they haven't, they will in time.

When I mention "time", I refer to the timing that God has

for them. There is no time limit with God and He forgives when we come to Him with a contrite spirit, and ask His forgiveness, and when we endeavor to do His will by following the reading of His word and obeying Him, He will forgive us.

There is a song titled, "Trust and obey, for there's no other way, to be happy in Jesus, but to trust and obey." I have found this to be so true. You can too.

My grandma Yates was the matriarch of the family. She made sure everything was right for all of us.

I'd love going to grandma Yates' house because I would get full attention from her. I know grandparents aren't supposed to have favorite grandkids but everyone knew I was her favorite.

She would constantly be doting over me. Seeing if I was sleeping, trying to feed me every hour (explains my fatness), but she'd always try to make sure I could do things by myself.

She would teach me how to scoot off the couch without hurting myself, and she knew before my mom that I could defend myself.

According to my grandmother, when I was around 3-4 years old, my little sister used to pull my hair. My mom wanted to spank Kim for doing it but my grandmother said "No he'll learn to defend himself."

So 1 day apparently I was talking really sweet to my little sister and told her to come closer because I had a secret. When my sister got real close I head butted her real hard.

According to Grandma, no more hair pulling after that. Hehehe Grandma was right.

She was fantastic at cooking. Back in the early 70's while my family was in Alaska, I was in the hospital in Grand Rapids Michigan getting new artificial prosthesis.

My mom arranged it to where grandma and grandpa would

come up from Indianapolis to pick me up from the hospital take me back to Indy for two weeks of love and attention then I would fly back to Alaska with my aunt Billie.

Even though there were only four people in the house grandma would cook as if it was a holiday every day. I loved it.

The company she worked for Western Electric had a group called Pioneers of America.

This group designed and built me my very first electric wheelchair. In the picture, on page 75, you will see two joysticks. There is one on each side.

I would use my shoulders to move each joystick. One joystick would be an accelerator/brake while the other joystick would be my steering mechanism. When I moved the joystick up, the chair would go forward, and when I moved the joystick down, the chair would move in reverse. I could also move it left and right.

As you see it was combination fire truck and convertible. That chair started me on my way to independence.

When I had the idea for this book, I immediately went to my grandma for her point of view. The only request I had was for her to be honest.

On Thanksgiving she wanted to read me what she wrote. I immediately heard my aunt Billie saying, no this is not the time to do it mother. My grandma sternly said "this is what he wanted. He wants me to be honest." She read to me what turned out to be the beginning of this chapter. I could see concern on everyone's faces. They thought I was going to be upset at her because she questioned God on why he put this burden on her daughter and if it's God's will to remove the burden.

Was I upset? No way. In fact I turned to my grandma and

gave her a big kiss. I thanked her because she did get it. Why would I be upset if someone felt that way?

If my child had a disabled child, I'd probably have done the same thing no matter how devout I am to the Lord. I wish to thank you grandma for caring so much and for getting it right.

# 10

## Grandpa Yates

*Grandpa Yates*

This is my grandfather on my mom's side of the family. He's the only grandpa I knew and loved because my dad's father died before I was born. Also, grandpa Yates was my father figure role model. As I stated growing up my dad was a heavy drinker and belligerent. Grandpa Yates was the exact opposite.

Grandpa Yates was the main influence in my love of sports. When we visit on holidays, while my siblings would play outside with the neighborhood children, my grandpa would take me and we either watched sports on television or he would show me his University of Kentucky memorabilia and talk to me how great UK Basketball was and in general college basketball.

He would tell me when he went to the University of Kentucky. Basketball was not about big money, shoe contracts or selfishness. The players did it for the love of the game and the fans would reciprocate that love by endlessly cheering.

Even though he showed me all these memories and told me all these stories it wasn't until 1985 when I fully understood. I went to my first UK game. UK vs. IU. As soon as I entered Rupp Arena, I understood. I just sat there in the wheelchair section soaking in the atmosphere. I looked up to heaven and said to my grandpa, you're right it's basketball at it's puresness.

A couple of weeks later I was asked to work for the UK wheelchair Basketball team. When the coach pushed me to the scorer's table showed me which buttons to press and when to press them, I nearly started to cry. I again looked up to heaven and told grandpa, "I made it, I really made it I'm working for the University of Kentucky."

When my grandpa died in 1982 it was the most difficult trauma for me to handle. Sure I nearly died a year before, my parents were divorced and my sister attempted suicide but his death was more severe to me. At the time he was my father figure. He was what a father should be. He was the first death of someone I loved and cared about. That Sunday morning I woke up with pain in my chest. Suddenly my mom entered the room with tears on her face and she told me grandpa had died. I love my grandparents and wish they were still here, but I'm glad that I have such fond memories of them and they'll always be in my heart.

# 11

## Aunt Shirley and Uncle Bill

Dear Kent,

I went through all my pictures and I couldn't find hardly anything. I lost a lot of pictures when Dave's basement flooded. I've been thinking back when you were born. I guess I'll never forget that day. When your dad called....We were in shock. Of course your dad said they told him; you would never make it. I'll never forget uncle Bill's reaction. He said it would be better if you didn't make it. I was so mad at him. All I knew was that I loved you no matter what. Well, you proved us wrong and I'm so glad because you are my favorite. I know you'll say I tell all of my nephews that.

Well, when you came home, Uncle Bill was kind of upset. He didn't know if he could see you. I told him he had better put his feelings aside. Anyway, when he saw you, you were so tiny but you had the cutest smile, and that head full of black hair. He loved you from that day on. Remember how you used to tease each other about having a big nose?

I'll always remember when he took you to get a haircut when you were staying with us. The barber refused to cut your hair, because he couldn't look at you. Uncle Bill was so mad at him, he never went back to him and neither did his boys. I remember your dad came home on leave and you came to visit. Remember the house on Vine Street? I had the upstairs and I couldn't find you. I looked and you were coming down the stairs hanging on with your chin. I panicked and you said, don't worry, I do it all the time. I always remember you were first "one of the kids" and the kids always included you.

I remember you liked the Chicago Bears. Mike was always a bear fan and he was always out at St. Joe when they trained there. I think you went out a time or two and watched them. Anyway that was when they got them to sign the football for you. He always wished he could have gotten you a ride with Coach Halas. Mike was out there so much a player gave him one of his practice jersey's. I can't remember which one it was. Mike wore that jersey day and night. Anyway, enough of that. Mike, Randy, and Terry always thought you were cool. I'll always' remember you laying on my living room floor with your head on Sheila, our dog. She would let you lay there for as long as you wanted to. As the years went on, you got older and the boys went to the Military Service or work. Debbie got married and had a little girl. You stayed with her off and on. Debbie said you were her babysitter when you were there. Melissa would get into something and you would yell for her. Remember when Melissa tried to take your drink. Deb said she never forgot that. Kent, you have brought a lot of love and joy into our lives. Our family would never have been complete without you. Randy and Terry said you always made all of us happy. No matter if we were down, you always made us smile.

I remember a special person in your life that you made smile when none of us could. That was Uncle Bill when he found out he had 6 months to live and you came up to the hospital and brought him a card and a mug with some candy. You looked at him and said, "uncle Bill, I believe your nose has gotten bigger." That started the teasing and a smile from him. I'll never forget. I remember you staying at the hospital when he went into surgery with me and the kids. Kent, I think you gave us more than we could ever give you. In our family, ;you are our hero.

Now, I want to say a few things about your family. Your MOM deserves the MOTHER OF A LIFETIME AWARD. I always said she deserved credit for everything you have accomplished, but after I read her book, I realized more of what she had done for you. I know your dad loved you and was proud of you. As you know, the last 2 or 3 years of his life was the brother I knew when we were growing up. He always said your mom deserved all the credit. Your grandpa Bell always said he wished he hadn't signed the paper for your dad to go the service. It made him grow up too fast. The war didn't help him any either.

I'm not making excuses for his drinking, but he always loved your mom. He never said anything bad about her and he told me in those last year he could not blame her. He said he wished he would have done things different. I'm sure your mom would agree with me. He was the old Sunny that he was a long time ago.

They say drinking is a disease. Well, you grandpa Bell's life was cut short due to drinking. He was only 52 years old. They say it runs in the family.

I can't remember much about you and grandma Bell. Probably because when you came to visit you were usually with me. Grandma was always there. You have 2 brothers and a sister that would always be there for you. I think you have enough cousins that would always be there also. Well, Kent, I can't think of much more to write about.

I just wanted to let you know how you being born has affected our family. We can't imagine you not being here.

This summer we are planning on having a family get together. We talked to Vic about it at Thanksgiving and he said him and Mary and all their kids would come. I'm hoping you will be able to come. And, Aunt Barb will be able to come. Tell Kim I love her and I'll talk to you later. Love you a lot.

Aunt Shirley

P.S. If there is anything else I can help you with give me a call. Anyway I want you to know we always looked forward to you coming home. You were never a burden on anybody. When the time came I could no longer lift you there were always the boys around to help and was glad to do it.

12

# The Hand of God

June 21st, 1981 I was in the hospital with a very serious Urinary Tract Infection. I was continuously bleeding from both ends of my body. Usually when I go to the hospital for an illness, I've had this attitude that I'll beat the illness and prove the doctors wrong. In 1981, I did not have that feeling. I wanted to die, I wanted out.

At 4:25 p.m. On June 21st, 1981 a friend from school had just left. When she closed the door, I knew it was my time to die. I closed my eyes and said: "Ok God, take me out of here, I'm ready." At that moment, I heard a voice say:

"You're going to live." I quickly opened my eyes, looked around the room, nobody was in the room, the TV was off and the radio was off. I thought I was hallucinating from my illness, IV Tubes and medication. I again laid my head down, closed my eyes and told God to take me.

For the second time the voice responded: "You're going to live." When I opened my eyes the second time, on the ceiling over my head appeared a silhouette of a hand like a shadow.

The hand then descended from the ceiling and covered my entire face. I did not see a tunnel of light nor did I see any relatives, even though it was in the afternoon in mid July when the hand covered my face all I could see was darkness. However, when the hand did cover my face I felt a soothing warmth inside of me. As if this hand was filling me up with nice warm water. I did not feel my tubes inside me. I did not feel the bed I was laying on. I felt as if I was in a nice warm bath.

Then a knock came on the door. I looked at the clock and only 5 minutes had passed. Into the room was my mom, my grandparents and my brother Daniel.

When they entered the room I was scared to say what had happened because I was only 16 and did not understood what had just occurred.

After my family left a nurse came into the room to change my bandages. I asked her to give me my bible for me to read. The nurse asked me if there was a specific scripture I wanted to read. I said, "no, I will just read the first thing I see." She opened the bible and placed it for me to read and the first scripture I saw was Psalms 102. The Prayer For The Afflicted:

1. Hear my prayer, O LORD, and let my cry come unto thee.
2. Hide not thy face from me in the day when I am in trouble; incline thine ear unto me: in the day when I call answer me speedily.
3. For my days are consumed like smoke, and my bones are burned as an hearth.
4. My heart is smitten, and withered like grass; so that I forget to eat my bread.
5. By reason of the voice of my groaning my bones cleave to my skin.
6. I am like a pelican of the wilderness: I am like an owl of the desert.

7. I watch, and am as a sparrow alone upon the house top.
8. Mine enemies reproach me all the day; and they that are mad against me are sworn against me.
9. For I have eaten ashes like bread, and mingled my drink with weeping.
10. Because of thine indignation and thy wrath: for thou hast lifted me up, and cast me down.
11. My days are like a shadow that declineth; and I am withered like grass.
12. But thou, O LORD, shall endure for ever; and thy remembrance unto all generations. (KJV)

As soon as I read those first five words I knew that God's hand touched me and healed me from the urinary tract infection and it was God who said, "You're going to live." Even though I knew God wanted me to live I wondered why he wanted me to live.

At that time, I thought God wanted me to live to inspire others by using my disability in a positive manner. I believed that for 21 years.

Then starting in 2002 God answered my question by showing me the first of two miracles which were explained in the chapter about my dad.

# 13

## Euphimisms and Disabilities

Yes, George Carlin did this but I love it so much I want to include it in my book. In the 1st world War a soldier's nervous system becomes so stressed that it snaps. They called it Shell shock. WWII Same condition was called Battle Fatigue. In the Korean War it was called Operational Exhaustion. In the Vietnam War the very same condition was called Post Traumatic Stress-Disorder. The pain was buried under the Jargon. If they call it Shell Shock today a lot more veterans would be helped.

The same thing would apply with disabilities. 1st is crippled. What's wrong with the word cripple? It's in the bible. "Jesus healed the cripples." Then it was the Physically Challenged. Then they used Differently Abled, Then handicapable. People think if you change the NAME of the condition it'll change the condition. Wrong. Just because you call me by any of those terms does not mean I'm going to walk or play basketball.

They're just words.

A woman came up to me at my job in Indianapolis and asked me "What do I call you?" I replied "Excuse me?" She said and I quote: "You people have different terms to call yourselves." I looked at her and said: "My name is Kenton, that's the name my parents gave me. All those so called terms are just words."

However, there is one term I really despise and if I see that Senator I'm running his butt down with my wheelchair. Daniel

Inuoye, Sen. D-HAWAII during a speech while unveiling the FDR statue to honor the ADA used this term.

"Tragically Afflicted"

1st Sen. Inouye is disabled himself. He was severely wounded in WWII. When I heard him use that term I immediately called his Washington office and told the receptionist how disgusted I was with that term and said "my disability is not a tragedy, and the only thing I'm afflicted with is intelligence not to use such terms."

I admit that I've done some amazing things, but when all is said and done, I'm still in this wheelchair. It would be like someone calling you different terms like hispanic, latino, or some others but in the end you are still Patty or Patricia.

Society needs to get off this labeling kick and accept each other as who we are. We are humans, God's creatures, individuals, not labels. Personally, you can call me anything you want just don't call me late for dinner.

14

# Howe Time Flies

This chapter is solely on the great times I had attending Thomas Carr Howe High School in Indianapolis from the years 1979-1983.

High school can either be the greatest four years of someone's life or the worst years. I personally felt it was the greatest times of my life and yes high school has prepared me in life.

Here's what I said to the football team in a pep talk I gave just before our class' 25th year reunion this September on how High school can be the building block for the rest of your lives.

Please always remember, whatever you do here at Howe whether it be in the classroom or on the field HOWE will be the launching pad for the rest of your life. Yes classroom will determine your future. Let me explain. Just like a job, your teachers give you assignments.

How well and how prompt you do that work determines what grades you'll get.

In the work field our grades are paychecks. The better work, the higher grade/paycheck.

Continuing to do a great job in the class room the better grades you get and at the end of the year you get promoted. Just like a career. So, whether your here at Howe or you're in the work force, the better your work, the more successful you'll be.

I've been blessed to have forged some lifelong friendships in high school that continue today. Those friends and stories will be in this chapter.

Yes, sweet little me got in trouble with Mr. Tout. I had a pair of artificial arms that I brought to school one day. (picture attached). As you see in the photo the hands looked real.

I could not electronically move the fingers but with assistance from a fellow student we moved the middle finger to the upright position. As per any good prank unfortunately, Mr. Tout saw my middle finger and told me to put it down. I told him somebody put my finger like that and I couldn't move it.

So Mr. Tout had to manually fix my hand to put my finger down. I also got in trouble with Ms. Amani when I skipped typing class.

## MY FIRST AND ONLY SO CALLED "DATE."

It starts on the last Friday night in September 1981. I was home talking on the phone to Debbie Babbs. There were two strange things about this night.

The first strange thing was, it was unusually quiet for a Friday night. Normally, my parents were arguing or if they went out, my siblings and I would have our friends over for a party. However, this Friday night it was very, very quiet.

The second strange thing was that Debbie was home talking to me. A good looking and smart girl like her you'd figure wouldn't be home.

So we were talking on the phone and my mom was playing the organ. Apparently, Debbie had a keyboard in her room because she was playing along with my mom and I was having this stereo effect.

After my mom was done playing, Debbie asked me if I knew

how to play any songs using the buttons on the phone. I told her no. She then proceeded to try and teach me Mary had a little lamb. After that song Debbie did the coolest thing I ever heard.

She pressed the following buttons on her phone. 321 21. Go ahead try it I'll wait.... Recognize the tune? It's "Riding the storm out" by REO Speedwagon. At the age of 16 I thought it was the coolest thing I've ever heard.

She then asked me if I knew how to play the piano/organ. I told her yes. My mom taught me two songs, When the Saints Go Marching in and Silver Bells. I can still play them. Debbie asked me if those were the only songs I knew and I said yes. Then all of a sudden without thinking I asked Debbie if she could come over and teach me more songs. She asked: "When?" I replied: "Tomorrow?" She then asked: "What time?" I answered: 2:00.

Her reply was "Sure." I never heard that from a woman before and I was so surprised that I said: "What?" She repeated it and asked me for directions to my house. I gave her the directions thanked her and told her see you tomorrow.

After I hung up the phone I told my mom that Debbie was coming over tomorrow. Mom's response was: "Oh, she probably just said that just to be nice." The next day, I told my mom to get me dressed for Debbie.

My mom didn't believe it. Well, 2:00 P. M. Arrived and a knock was on the front door. All of a sudden my mom ran into my room and said: "Kent, there's a girl here to see you!" I responded: "That's what I've been telling you since last night!" So mom had to hurry and get me dressed. I cannot remember the songs Debbie tried to teach me but at that time I didn't care because she was the only girl I asked out and she said yes. That was good enough for me.

A month after that, I decided to try and press my luck

and ask Debbie out again. This time it was going to be to the Homecoming football game and dance.

I actually planned this out with my brother and his wife. If Debbie said yes, my brother and his wife would've driven me to Debbie's house picked her up, all 4 of us go to dinner, then to game and dance and my brother and his wife would be our chaperones.

Stupid me: I waited two days before homecoming to ask. By that time somebody else had asked her. Now before you start feeling sorry for me there is a positive spin to this. Debbie must have noticed that I was really nervous about asking her out. After gently saying no she said something to me that changed my approach to asking women out.

Debbie said: "Don't be afraid to ask me again." I went home and thought about that. I thought. What do I have to be afraid of? All they can do is say no. If they say no, move on to the next one. Ever since, I've not been afraid to ask a woman out. Thank you, Debbie for bringing out my confidence.

# 15

## Melisa- Howe High School

January 1982. The Boys Basketball team was playing at Arlington. It was the channel 4 high school game of the week. I was sitting between the team bench and the lovely cheerleaders. There was a camera man roaming the sidelines.

During a pause in the action, our section was yelling at the camera man to video us. When he turned around and that red light went on, Melisa Petree put her arms around me and gave me a big kiss on my right cheek.

I had two reactions. 1st reaction was the Austin Powers "Yea Baby!" reaction. My second reaction was crap. Nobody is going to see this because no one in my family watched channel 4 except for Sammy Terry and Cowboy Bob.

Well, my dad picked me up from the game. That in itself was very, very rare.

Here's how rare it was for my dad to pick me up. That 1 time. Usually, it was my mom first, then my 2 brothers then if they couldn't they would send my brother's friend Jim then if he couldn't do it, I'd ask a friend from school who had a car then only as a last resort my dad would pick me up. Back then dad and I didn't have much interaction.

Anyway, as we were driving home my dad asked me: "Who was that pretty girl with her arms around you and kissing you." I said: "You saw that?" My dad smiled and told me he was watching the game to see when it was over so he could pick me up. Duh, I told him she was in my Spanish class.

Side note: Even though choir had some really hot ladies I.E. Claire, Yvonne Golden, Sarah Clark, Julie (Bankston) Edens and others, that Spanish class of 81-82 was the class for Howe Honeys. Karen (Clubs) Kottkamp, Debbie Babbs, Melisa Petree, Lisa Pearcy, Lisa Cosby, Lisa LaRue, Juanita Do'nofrio and of course Sherri (Dockery) Davis.

That was a teenage boy's dream class. (Maybe I crossed the line? NAH!!!!!) My dad asked me if we were dating, I told him no. He replied, "You should she's cute." I never asked her out. I didn't want to press my luck. One of the few bonding moments between my father and I during my teenage years.

When I turned 18 my dad told me that before he saw the cheerleader kissing me, that he was worried about me attracting women because of my disability. If he did not see her kiss me my dad was going to hire a hooker for my 18$^{th}$ birthday.

But when my dad did see that I would have no problem with the ladies he was happy. So thank you Melisa for saving me the embarrassment.

# 16

## Scott and Kent

During high school I had a "Twin" brother or so everybody thought we were. His name is Scott Bell. We are the same age. He loved sports like me and had beautiful women around him just like me. There were only two differences.

First, we did not look alike and second we were not even related but we had fun with it to the point that 1 day he, his sister Tammy and I got together and adopted each other as brothers and sister.

We figured hey everybody thinks we're related let's make it unofficially official that we are.

This "twin" confusion came to a head during a basketball

pep rally when accidentally Scott and I switched identities for a day.

During the pep Rally, Coach Jake Thompson would introduce each player as they dribbled down the court and either made a jump shot, layup or dunk. Since Scott was the captain of the team he was the last player introduced.

As he was dribbling down the court, the coach accidentally called him "Kent Bell!" When Scott heard my name instead of his, he stopped and looked at me as if he was going to pass me the ball. I was asking him to do it but he thought better, continued down the court made the jumper and exited the gym.

This is where it gets funnier and unplanned. After the pep rally, I went to the coach and told him of his mistake the coach didn't believe me until four other students agreed with me.

At that time Scott was dating a lovely cheerleader Karen Clubs who was in my Spanish class. After the pep rally, Karen walked over to me and said to me "Hey Scott." Kissed me and placed her books in my lap and proceeded to push me to my next class. As we were going to class we see the real Scott Bell and he says to me: "Hey Scott Hey Karen." We both replied to him "Hey Kent." For one day I was glad to be Scott Bell and not Kent Bell because for that one day, I was with the cheerleader.

# 17

# My College Years Part 1

## 1983-84 BALL STATE

Through most of my education years, I went to "Mainstreamed" schools. "Mainstream" Is where schools would place students with disabilities into the abled bodied population. You younger readers may think that was all the time but before the Rehab Act of 1973 and the ADA of 1990, Students with disabilities were segregated into completely separate and in most cases lower standard schools.

Even in Alaska before the Rehab Act was signed I was mainstreamed.

The only times I wasn't mainstreamed was in 1st and 2nd grades in Virginia where they sent me a tutor at home. That was fun because my sister who was not old enough to go to school would sit in with me and she got advanced learning. The other was in 8th grade. Even after the Rehab Act was signed 5 years earlier, just like the ADA, local cities were very slow or in defiance of the laws and in 1978 I was forced to go to a non mainstreamed school.

In the beginning of the school year I thought it was great because I got A'S & 100% on most of my tests. It wasn't until a mid-year bus ride I realized why I was so smart.

On the bus there was a girl named Tamika. She was 4 years

younger than me and she was in a wheelchair. On Tamika's lap were her books. I noticed her math book looked a lot like mine. I asked her what was the green book?

She lifted it up to show me that even though she was 4 years younger than me we were learning the same thing.

Then it dawned on me that the reason I kept getting great grades was not because I was so smart, the reason was that I was being taught lower educational skills that I already knew 4 years ago.

When I realized that I was doing 4$^{th}$ grade work even though I was supposed to be in 8$^{th}$ grade I would do my assignments ahead of schedule but unfortunately was now being bored and unchallenged.

This came to a head during the year end parent teacher conference. Even though my grades were fantastic and I was continuously on the Honor Roll this 1 teacher (for legal reasons I'll call Ms. D.) Recommended that I'd be held back from going to a mainstream high school and instead go through their so-called "high school" program.

She went as far as saying and I quote "By the time he's 16 he'll drop out of school and be a complete failure."

That's right, a teacher calling a student a COMPLETE FAILURE. That pissed off my mom and I to no end.

My mom had to write an appeal letter to the IPS Superintendent showing my grades to get me out of that place.

When the School board saw my excellent grades they agreed. I found out 10 years later why this 1 school was always holding students back.

I found out that the school was receiving government money for every student. So the longer they had a student the longer they'd kept their funding. How did I find this out?

Well, when the other students parents saw how my mom fought for me to go to a mainstream school they decided to pull their kids out of there. The school was eventually closed due to lack of funding. Coincidence?

Through my high school years those two words "COMPLETE FAILURE" stuck in me so much I wanted to prove that teacher wrong. In my senior year I not only proved her wrong but God arranged it where I got to actually shove it right down her throat face to face. Two weeks from graduation that "Special school" was taking some of their students through my high school.

Well, guess who was a chaperone? That's right the wicked witch her-self.

During my lunch hour I was invited to talk to these students about my experiences in high school. I was too happy to accept.

After talking to the kids about high school, I saw that dreaded teacher standing alone. I decided that now was my time for redemption.

I approached her calmly and said: "Ms. D.?" She nodded. I then said: "Do you remember 4 years ago you recommended me that I not come to this high school because you said and I quote, 'By the time he turns 16 he'll be a high school drop-out and a COMPLETE FAILURE'?" She nervously said yes. I looked on my lap and I had my graduation invitation.

I continued: "Well, I'm 18 I haven't dropped out, I'm two weeks from graduation AND I just received a $500 scholarship to Ball State University. Here's an invitation to my graduation. How's that for a COMPLETE FAILURE?" I left without allowing her to respond. I was so happy that after 4 years I got redemption.

I called my mom and told her what happened. My mom said she wished she had known in advance so she could have been there because she wanted to punch that teacher in the face. I told my mom no, it was better this way because this was my battle. When I got to my next class I was smiling so much my teacher thought I've been smoking pot. I told her no, and I explained why I was smiling. After my explanation the class was cheering.

So, to Ms. D. or, to any teacher, I have one piece of advice. Please don't call anybody a "COMPLETE FAILURE" without first giving them a chance to fail.

# 18

# My College Years Part 2

## LEXINGTON COMMUNITY AND THE UNIVERSITY OF KENTUCKY 1985-89

After graduating from high school, I was excited about moving out of the house and going to college. (cue shattered illusion effect). My first attempt at college was miserable. Oh I had fun. But unfortunately I had waaaaayyyyy too much fun. Every weekend I'd go out with a different girl, partied too hard and drank too much. What made it worse that since these girls would talk to me made their boyfriends so jealous that they would play sick "Jokes" on me and my room-mate.

As my friends know I do like practical jokes as long as they're in good clean (sort of) fun. These so-called "Jokes" however were far over the line. The worst "joke" was when two guys put dead rats in my electric wheelchair. That's right dead rats and not the plastic kind either. I told the Dorm head about it but his response was since no witnesses saw exactly who did it he couldn't do anything.

My room-mate decided we'll take care of this ourselves. I accused one of the suspects. His reply: "Did you see me do it?" I replied "No." He then said, "You can't accuse me of something I didn't do." Well, my room-mate decided to keep the dead rats in a plastic bag. I didn't realize that he had retribution in his mind.

When the two evil doers went to lunch they left their door

unlocked. My job was to be the warning scout in case they returned. My room-mate then got the plastic bag of dead rats, went into the other room and strategically placed the rats in their room. When I said strategically, I mean he would place 1 rat each under the pillows, a rat in each shoe, some in the closet and some on their desk.

One of the guys returned after we finished. When he saw the "Pets" in his room he yelled my name. I entered the hallway and he told me he didn't like what I did. I responded with: "Did you see me do it?" He replied "No." I then said, ".You can't accuse me of something I didn't do." Which technically I didn't do it, my room-mate did. (thanks Bill) As I was leaving the hall, I purposely swerved my electric wheelchair at him and the corner edge of my lap board went into his "family jewels." As I continued trapping him against the wall I told him "Never f### with me again or you'll never have children."

Now everything at Ball State was not bad. As I said, I had waaayyyy too much fun. 1st I experienced the Rocky Horror Picture Show nine straight Saturday nights. Lost my virginity at BSU, participated in a bed race, but these next two were the best.

Before my neighbors turned evil they were actually fun people who listened to great music such as The Dead Kennedys and Yaz. On Halloween they even helped me with my costume. They were theatre students and they had great props and makeup. I decided to be a military POW.

I got an old t-shirt and the 2 theatre students got some fake blood and put it on the shirt where my arms were supposed to be. Then we wrapped a towel around my bottom and put the fake blood on the towel where my legs were supposed to be. We let it dry then since the girls dorms was inside the same complex as ours I didn't have to go outside.

When it dried I laid on the floor and rolled through the girls dorms trick or treating while my room-mate followed me pointing a machine gun at me as if he captured me. When the girls answered the door you should've seen their reactions.

My next is probably my favorite. Near Christmas 1983 this girl asked me what I wanted for a present, as a joke I said "A pair of mittens." A couple of days later I saw her knitting. I asked her what she was knitting and she said with a grin: "Your mittens." The dorm Christmas party was starting and I had my friends put me in a box then they wrapped the box in Christmas decorations and carried the box with me inside to the party.

When the gifts were being exchanged the girl asked where was I? My room-mate said I was not feeling well and I had the guys deliver her present in a big box. When she opened the box, I said "MERRY CHRISTMAS!" Yes she was shocked. But then she got me back because she did give me a pair of homemade mittens in my favorite color and she even stitched my name on each mitten. I still have those mittens and every Christmas I hang them on my tree. Thank you Lisa.

Yes, if you want to party go to Ball State. If you want to study, go anywhere else. Here's how bad my grades at Ball State were. Out of a possible 4.0 GPA My GPA was 0.8. That's right I couldn't even muster a 1.0 GPA. My best grade happened to be in my hardest class with whom everybody called was the toughest professor at Ball State. I liked him. He was a refugee from Hungry when Russia invaded Hungary and turned it into a communist regime.

Every time the professor would get a parking ticket from the campus police we would hear about it in class and he would compare the campus police to the Russian Soldiers as he would re tell his story of getting out of Hungry during the invasion.

This scenario would happen once a week through the entire semester. Fun class. When I would take the tests I had to go to his office and it was an oral exam. For someone who was supposed to be mean and evil I found to be a nice guy.

After flunking out of Ball State I was miserable. I had no direction and I had no clue what to do, I actually thought my 8th grade teacher might be right I might be a complete failure. In the summer of 1985 my friend from high school Kirk Huehls called me and invited me for a week's vacation with him and his wife down in Nicholasville, Ky. I decided sure. Maybe a change of scenery might cheer me up. Little did I know that change of scenery would alter my life for the better.

Kirk picks me up from a summer camp I was at. When we get to Nicholasville, Kentucky, I noticed how peaceful it was and how pretty it was. During my stay Kirk asked me if I wanted to live with them, go to school at the University of Kentucky. He said he and his wife would take care of me.

I was very hesitant. I didn't know whether or not my mom would allow me to move so far away. Also, I only had one class in high school with Kirk so really, hardly knew him. But, as Kirk puts it. What have I got to lose? I was doing nothing in

Indiana, depressed at my situation so literally this might be my last chance to turn my life around. I agreed.

The biggest hurdle or so I thought was trying to convince my mom. I waited until she picked me up from Kentucky and we were going back to Indy to spring this on her. As we were between Cincinnati & Indy I decided to ask her. I said: "Mom what would you think if I wanted to move down to Kentucky live with Kirk and his wife and go to school at UK?"

My mom shocked me with this answer: "If you had called me last night and told me this then I would've left you down there and sent your stuff down later." I was floored. My mom was thrilled for me to live in Kentucky. Her dad went to UK so she was thinking that I was carrying on the family tradition. When I got to Indy I called Kirk and told him, "yes I can move to Kentucky."

I went back to Kentucky the Sunday before classes started. That following day, Kirk drove me to UK for me to enroll. However, when they saw my Ball State grades, UK said no and advised me to try and go to Lexington Community College to get my grades up. So we went to LCC and their disabled Student Advisor Frances Hunter was sooo great in helping me with registration, admission and financial aid. She scheduled my classes all in one day. So even though I was an LCC student my student ID said University of Kentucky because LCC was part of the UK System. So, technically, I'm in UK.

Classes were much better at LCC. Teachers and advisors really did care about the students.

# 19

## Patricia Puebla

Patricia & I met in 1985 at Lexington Community College. We had some classes together but it wasn't until a last minute request on my part to go to a concert where we actually started to become friends. My Roommate Kirk Huehls and I bought two tickets to see John Mellencamp at Rupp Arena. Kirk was going to drive me. Well, at the last minute Kirk tells me he can't go because he had to work so he sold me his ticket and left it up to me to get my own ride.

So there I was stuck with two tickets but no way to get there. I was in the lobby and I could have asked anybody to go because these were floor seats. Somehow, I see Patty sitting in the lobby and I just decided what the heck? I approached her and said: "Hey, I have two floor seats to John Mellencamp tonight but Kirk bailed out on me and I have no ride. I know it's the last minute and if you have other plans don't sweat it, but if I give you a ticket can you give me a ride to the show?" She said sure but I would have to meet her at the Student Center for dinner.

I thought great, how am I going to get to the Student Center in my manual wheelchair? Well, I asked another friend to drive me to the Student Center. I get there and we have dinner. Then it's off to Rupp Arena for the show. We get to the floor level. However, they won't allow my wheelchair into the floor seating area because the stage design was so big that there was no wheelchair seating on the floor for this particular show. Without hesitation and without me asking, Patty lifts me out of my wheelchair and begins to carry me to my seat. (that scenario would play out again in the battle with Medicaid, so stay tuned). Before we leave the backstage area Patty tells the security Guard: "If anything happens to that wheelchair we'll sue."

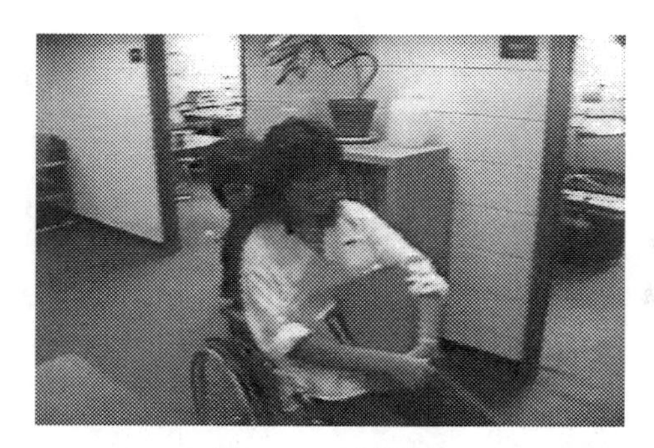

*Patty and Kent*

She carries me to my seat. The concert begins but problem number two occurs. Since I'm so short when everybody stands up I cannot see. So, wonderful Patty lifts me up to try and see over everybody. I'll be the first to tell you, I'm not light to lift so it was difficult for her to hold me high enough to see without her arms getting tired. Well, about halfway through the show Patty's brilliant mind came up with a great idea.

Patty carried me from our seats and we went directly to the front and she sat me on the lower tier of the stage and put her hands on my back so I wouldn't fall. That's right, I got to sit partially on stage and security did nothing to stop us. That's one of the great things about Patty. When she makes her mind up to do something she does it with conviction and nothing or nobody will stop her not even concert security guards. :D

It wasn't until some months after that concert where Patty

became not only a great friend but she turned into one of the most wonderful persons I've been blessed to meet. I could give you every superlative to describe how wonderful she was to me, but to me the best way to describe her is this. If you need one person to take with you to a fight and you really needed someone to be there when the odds are against you, Patty is the perfect friend.

This next story about Patty shows how good of a friend she is and if she takes charge of a situation things get done.

Here is some background information so you will understand the next major problem I had to go through.

Every 5 years, Medicaid/Medicare allows me the opportunity to apply for a new electric wheelchair.

Here's how the process goes. First, I take the forms to my doctor and my doctor has to verify that I'm disabled enough to need an electric wheelchair. That's right according to Medicaid/ Medicare I'm not disabled unless a doctor says I am. I'm not exaggerating.

Then after the doctor fills out the forms they're sent to Medicaid/Medicare where depending on when it's received and how back logged the caseworker is with other clients the papers sits on their desk until the caseworker gets to it and puts the information into the computer system.

Once it's in the system, the supervisor again. depending on case load, will look at the info and either approve or deny my application. If denied (which does happen) I have to go through a long appeal process. If approved the supervisor will call the local wheelchair store and tell them to order the wheelchair. Measurements are taken. Then the local store calls the manufacturer and have the parts shipped to Kentucky where the store assembles the chair then delivers it. In a perfect world this process can take up to 6 months, but if you have any knowledge of the system, nothing with Medicaid/Medicare is close to perfect.

Since my dad was in the Army I've learned that all paper work must be in triplicate. (3 copies) Dealing with Medicaid/ Medicare I know why. Before the caseworker could put my information into the system she lost my papers not once but twice. When I found out that my papers were lost for the second time, I exploded. I admit I have a temper but when I rely on someone else and they fail in their duties two times I go on a terror. I was in the lobby of the school just ranting and raving about how incompetent the system is.

Patty was coming out of class and she heard me yelling so she approached me and asked me what's wrong. I tell her that those (expletives) at Medicaid lost my paperwork again. She asked me if I had any more copies and I replied "yes." I have one last copy at the house. She then asked me where the Medicaid Office was. I told her it's in Frankfort, Kentucky. She asked me for the address and I told her it's on the papers. She calmly said to me: "Don't ride the bus tomorrow. I'll pick you up." I looked at her confused and she told me again, not to ride the bus she'll pick me up and we'll take care of this. Little did I know it wasn't "WE'LL take care of this" it was more of "SHE'LL" take care of this.

The next morning sure enough, Patty was at the house. We get the paperwork and we headed out to Frankfort. KY. As we are on the road I advise Patty since I didn't have a "scheduled" appointment we would have to wait until someone cancels or if someone doesn't show up for their appointment. This could mean, we might be there for hours. Patty says: "Even if we have to come back tomorrow we're getting this taken care of." Then

Patty says to me: "Kent let me do the talking." I asked her why? She tells me; "Because I can see that you're still upset and I'm afraid you might say something that will have them reject you." She was right. I was still upset. I was thinking however, what could Patty say to them that would solve this? It wasn't her words but her actions that convinced me.

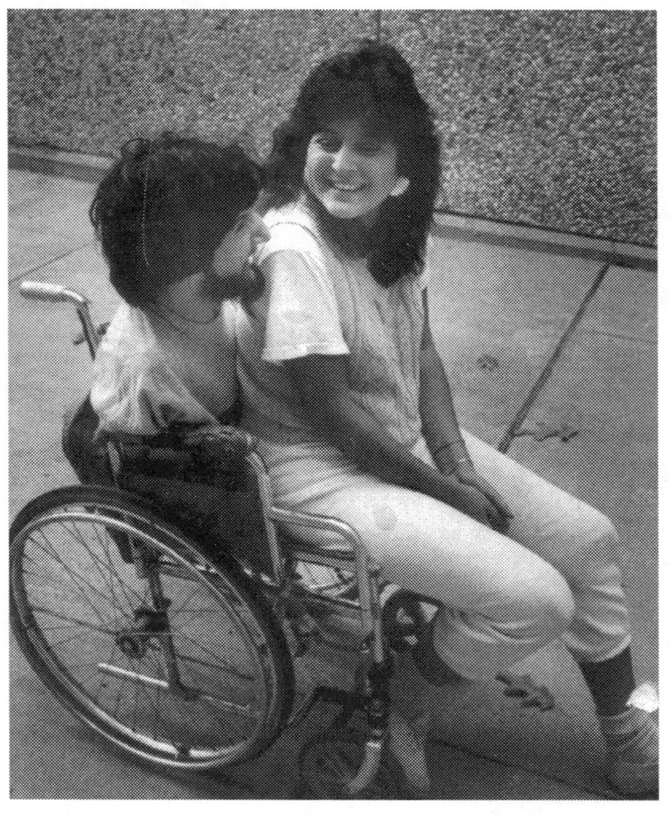

*Kent and Patty*

We get to the office, and sign in. Luckily we only had to wait 45 minutes for them to call my name. Usually, when you have a meeting with a caseworker it takes about 30 minutes. Not if you have Patty on your side.

Here's exactly what happens. Patty pushes me right up to the caseworker's desk. Then without saying a word, Patty picks me up out of my wheelchair and sits me on the woman's desk just so the caseworker can get a close up view on how disabled I am. Then Patty places my paperwork on the desk and tells the caseworker: "Don't you think he needs an electric wheelchair? I do." Then Patty takes me off the desk, puts me back in my wheelchair and as we are leaving the office Patty says: "Oh, that's his last copy of his paperwork, Don't lose it." Then we leave. This took less than 5 minutes. We get into the car and I'm laughing my butt off. The look on the caseworker's face when I was on her desk was priceless. In fact I didn't care if I got the wheelchair or not just seeing the shocked look was good enough for me. As I stated the process usually takes six months but after Patricia's brilliant presentation that six months was magically reduced to two weeks.

That's right, after I sat on that woman's desk she decided to cut through the BS and I got my chair within two weeks. So if you have a problem with Medicaid/Medicare, I suggest two things. 1st. Go directly to them and embarrass them. 2nd. Get a great friend like Patty to speak on your behalf. Yes the 2nd part is more difficult because friends like her are very, very rare.

I affectionately call this Patty and Bono. I was only an innocent bystander in this event. It actually begins on Oct 3rd 1987 when tickets were going on sale for the Oct. 23rd 1987 U2 concert in Lexington Ky. Tickets were to go on sale at 9 am. I could not camp over night so I gave money to a friend of mine who was camping out to hopefully get me tickets. This was during "The Joshua Tree" tour which at that time was their best selling album and tour. So going to see U2 live was the "thing".

When the box office opened, a human stampede occurred

and fans got injured and my friend at that time was not able to get tickets due to the chaos. When Patty got to school she asked me if I had gotten tickets, I sadly said, "No." I asked her if she got tickets and she said no and she was hurt by the stampede. She was really depressed when neither of us got tickets.

An hour later a friend of mine named Jeff, came to me and said there are wheelchair seats still available. I asked him "How?" when the show was supposedly sold out within 5 minutes? Jeff told me that Rupp Arena held back all the wheelchair seating tickets from the original general public so us people in wheelchairs can get a fair shot. (As I stated in my "Free Bird" chapter, Rupp Arena treated persons with disabilities fabulously). I was ecstatic because now I had another chance. I went to my friend Karen and one of my wheelchair basketball players Rod Bobbitt. I gave them my money and told them to get me tickets. Karen and Rod thought each other was cute so I picked those two for possible match making.

When they returned I thought Karen was telling me she had gotten four tickets. I asked her how could you get 4 tickets for $40.00? She walked up to me pulled the tickets out and said: "No we got you FLOOR seats." I looked at Jeff and asked where was the wheelchair seating on floor level? He smiled and replied: "Front row."

I was amazed. An hour after the show was supposedly sold out, here I had front row tickets and I didn't have to go through a scalper. Now my only question was when to tell Patty. I knew I had to take Patty. She and I had an agreement. Whoever got tickets first, would take the other to the show. If both of us got tickets we would use the best seats and sell the others. Since I got the tickets, I had to take her even though it ticked off a lot of my friends. But a deal is a deal. If she found out that I had front row to U2 & didn't take her? Let's just say it would not have been pretty.

I waited a few days to tell her. Why? I don't know. Each day that passed by she was more and more saddened and gloomy. Finally I couldn't stand to see her so down so one day after class, I went to her and told her to take something out of my coat pocket.

Folks, when she saw that I had tickets you thought she just opened up an early Christmas present. It didn't compare to her excitement when I told her that they were front row. She went from Christmas present happy to winning the lottery exuberance. I wished I had a camera because it was a priceless moment.

Simultaneously, the local newspaper was writing a feature story about me going to school. They followed me everywhere including to the concert. When Patty and I got to the venue, the newspaper reporter and photographer followed us to our seats. The photographer was taking pictures while the reporter was writing my answers to her questions. I looked around us and saw that the crowd was looking at Patty and I. I wasn't sure if they were looking at us because there was a beautiful woman (Patty) was sitting in my wheelchair with me or they thought I was this big time celebrity with a photographer and reporter following me. Either reason I was soaking it all in.

We got to our seats and suddenly Patty turns quiet. Not usual, enjoying the concert quiet. This was statue, motionless quiet. During the entire opening act Patty just sat there lifeless. I thought something was wrong. Was I sooooo wrong. The lights went dark and U2 started with the song "Where The Streets Have No Name." On top of the speaker near us was a cup of water to which when Bono came out he kicked the water off the speaker and yes we got wet. Patty immediately leaped to her feet spun towards me hugged me and thanked me for the tickets.

Then it happened. It was almost like slow motion. Without saying a word Patty took off a necklace that had a cross on it that her mother gave her. Patty then stood up started walking towards the stage. Two security guards stepped in front of her to stop her. Bono sees what was happening. He walks over and tells security "it's ok." Patty hands Bono her necklace he kisses her hand thanks her and she returns to her seat.

It looked like Patty was in a trance because as she's walking to her seat she didn't realize that Bono held the necklace up to the crowd and says to everybody "This girl has just given me a necklace and I don't know what to do with it." Then he puts the necklace in his pocket. When I told her what Bono did she did not believe me until we got to her apartment and her room mates Leah and Cami confirmed it gleefully.

Usually this would end at that night. Oh no. A couple of months later, I'm at my mom's home watching MTV. They were showing Christmas videos and they were premiering U2's "(It's Christmas) Baby please come home". The video was shot in Baton Rouge Louisiana two weeks after the Lexington show. I saw in the video that Bono had two crosses around his neck, a short necklace with a cross and a longer shinier necklace with a cross on it. Guess who the shiny one was. I immediately called Patty at her parents' house in Connecticut.

I excitedly told Patty to turn on MTV now! She asks why? I replied "Your necklace!" In the distance I hear Patty yelling "OH MY GOD! HE'S WEARING MY NECKLACE!" So folks during Christmas when you see U2'S video, "(It's Christmas) Baby please come home", you'll see two crosses around Bono. The slightly longer and shinier cross is from my friend Patty.

I would like to thank you Bono for not discarding her necklace. The moments from those days will forever bring a smile to my heart as you showed class towards one of your most loyal fans.

Thank you Patty for you have brought me so many wonderful joys, and comfort to me. Those three years when we went to school will forever bring joy and happiness to me. I'm truly blessed that God brought you into my life.

Patty's comments: My friend has no arms or legs. He has inspired me since college. Although I helped him get around sometimes he helped me 1 million times more. He NEVER complained. I think about Kenton when I hear such simple yet deep quotes. Such as.....Whether you think you can or you can't, you're right!' is all in your mind":) I'm grateful I truly get this. Thanx Kenton:)

my favorite flavor of ice cream is chocolate

# 20

## Freebird

"What is it you want to hear?"
"FREE BIRD!"
I heard it that time

Alright folks kick back relax get your lighters out because we are going to talk about one special evening in October 1987. Actually that entire year was special. The local paper did a story on me, CBS News did a story about me and the concert scene in Lexington Kentucky was off the chain. In one year, I saw Pink Floyd, Van Halen, U2 and Lynyrd Skynyrd. All of them were front row.

Rupp Arena is the place for persons with disabilities to go to concerts. Depending on the stage design if you had floor seats and you were in a wheelchair? You go to the front row, no questions asked. Of course there was the exception, such as the John Mellencamp fiasco. But for the most part, people in wheelchairs were spoiled in Lexington.

A friend of mine Randy "Too tall" Jones was dating a DJ from the local rock station. She scored us some free tickets to the Skynyrd reunion concert. So, Randy, his girlfriend, "Downtown" John Brown, Charles Rust and I got into the Chuck mobile to head to the show. When we got there we found out we had floor seats and of course I got to go up to the front while the others had to sit twelve rows back.

As any of my wonderful friends who has taken me to concerts (Charles, Tabitha, Michele & Patty), knows that when I go to concerts I have a really, really good time. I admit, I dance in my chair head bang and just plain act like a fool. This night was no different.

After Skynyrd finished their main set and the crew was setting up for the encore, a member of the group approached me and gave me a picture of the band. I did not know until I saw Skynyrd's "Behind The Music" the guy was their drummer Artimus Pyle. I asked him if I can get it autographed just to prove to my friends and siblings that I didn't buy it. He asked me what my name was and I told him. So he took the picture backstage and a few minutes later returned and said: "I couldn't get them to autograph it for you, but we have something better in store for you." I was thinking to myself what could be better?

The band returned to the stage. The new singer Johnny Van Zant was carrying a hat his brother would wear while singing. Johnny Van Zant 1st started talking about how the song Free Bird was inspired by the death of Duane Allman in 1971. Then he was talking about the plane crash that killed his brother Ronnie, Guitarist Steve Gaines and backup singer Cassie Gaines. Then he talked about the men and women who are in the military, police and firefighting that sacrificed their lives to keep us safe.

Then it happened, near the end of his speech Johnny Van Zant said: "And this goes out to you Kent Bell, where are you Kent?" I'm jumping up and down in my wheelchair yelling here I am. I was jumping so much my friend David had to hold my chair down so I wouldn't fall over. Johnny Van Zant sees me and says "Oh there you are don't fall out of your chair man this song is for you."

At that time Johnny Van Zant refused to sing the words to Free Bird because it was so emotional. So what he did was that he took his brother's hat and placed it on the microphone stand. And He said to the crowd: "My brother was the only one in the group who could sing this perfectly, but since he's not here, YOU ALL KNOW THE WORDS, YOU SING IT!" So 15,000 people stood up and sang Free Bird while the band played along and it was for that brief 15 minutes, I can honestly say, FREE BIRD WAS MY SONG.

# 21

## My Time on the Oprah Winfrey Show

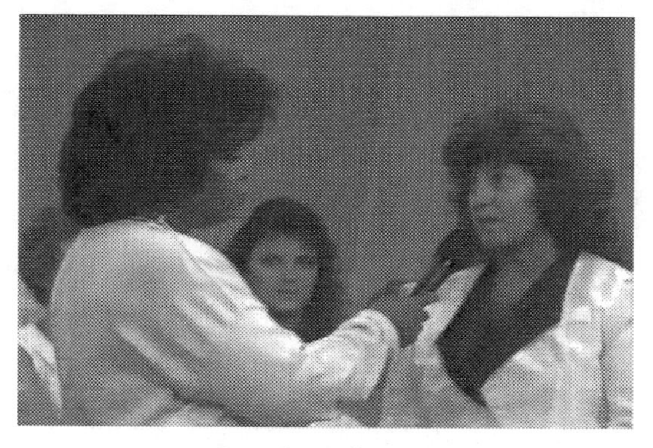

*Oprah and Mom*

This is literally a journey into the surreal and example of a dream coming true.

It begins in 1987 when the local newspaper and local television station in Lexington, Kentucky were doing feature stories about me going to college.

After the stories came out I got a call from a reporter in Boca Raton Florida. She was the sister of the Lexington newspaper reporter and saw the story. She wanted to do her own story about me for her publication: "The Globe." That's right the tabloid. I did not want to become a freak show so before I agreed I forced her to send me some of her work.

She sent me some of her stories, and I actually liked them. She wrote her story and stupid me did not ask for payment.

## LESSON 1.

Here's where it gets surreal. On August 4th 1988 I'm at my mom's house in Indianapolis. At 9 am she wakes me up to tell me I have a phone call from a lady in London England. Half groggy I answer it. This time it's a reporter for a publication called "News of the world." "The Sun"…Yes another tabloid only this tabloid had naked women in it.

According to the British reporter, She saw my story in "The Globe." And her publication and "The Globe" were owned by the same company.

Since I learned my lesson from "The Globe" this time I decided to seek payment from London. I told the reporter I wanted $800 before I would allow her to write her story.

She agreed to my terms. Little did I know $800 to them was chump change because this story went not only to London but I was receiving letters from Australia, South Africa and Hong Kong from people who received their countries version of the publication.

## LESSON 2.

After I hung up on the British reporter, I started laughing on how surreal it was talking to somebody across the ocean for a interview. I made a comment to my mom saying: "Maybe the queen will read this and invite me to England. My mom responded with, "Maybe Oprah will read it and have you on her show." I said to mom, "Why would Oprah read a tabloid from England?" My mom then told me that when the Lexington newspaper story came out she sent a copy to the show for a suggested topic.

Since my mom sent the story in November 1987 and here it was August 1988 we both laughed it off.

The next day I'm reading the Sunday paper. In the TV Weekly section, I was reading listings on tv shows. Mostly cartoons and sports.

This particular listing however, caught my attention. Wednesday August 8th 4:00 p.m. Channel 6 WRTV. Oprah Winfrey- Topic, Handicapped people and attitudes.

Usually when I see a listing like that, I avoid the program. Usually when you see a program that has handicapped (disabled) people, one of two things occur. Either the program is sooo sweet and positive that it rots your teeth. Or, on the other end is that the show is to negative and depressing you want to kill yourself.

For me my life has been right down the middle. Yes there are fantastic moments and yes, there have been some very bad moments. So, before August 5th 1988, I avoided these types of shows. However, when I read the listing for the Oprah show, I told my mom to call me and remind me to watch the show. My mom was surprised and said: "You hate those types of shows." I said: "I know but I feel I have to watch this one."

That night I had a dream of me being on the show.

*Oprah and Kent*

Monday August 6th. I woke up sick. Let's just say diarrhea. Around 2 pm my oldest brother Vic and his girlfriend (later wife) Mary came over to check on me while mom was at work.

Mary says to me there's a phone call for me and it's long distance. I thought it was either Patty or one of my friends in Kentucky. So I answer the phone: "Yello." The voice on other end says, "Hi, my name is Dianne Hudson and I'm a producer for the Oprah Winfrey show."

I must have been scared poopless because when my brother was leaving the house he turned to say bye and he saw my eyes popping out of my head because he asks: "What's wrong?" As the lady was talking, I said in the most excited voice. "It's the Oprah Winfrey Show man!" Vic was surprised as much as me and nearly fell down the steps as he was telling me good luck.

When my brother left I turned my attention back to the phone. The producer said they got the newspaper article that my mom sent. She stated they've been trying to contact me for six weeks. The show thought I lived in Lexington and were calling the house I stayed at during the school year. They did not know I would go back to mom's in Indianapolis for the summer. When the show called the house in Lexington one of the foster kids would just say Kent's not here and hang up.

Luckily, on August 6th the producer tried one last time. When she called Lexington this time my friend Kirk's mother, Judy answered the phone and told the producer I was at my mom's in Indy. Then she gave the producer my mom's phone number. All the stars were aligning themselves. Here it is two days before the show and on their final attempt they finally got in touch with me.

The producer, was describing how the show goes. In 1988 the Oprah show was similar to Phil Donahue. Oprah sometimes would have people call in to tell their stories and/or opinions. When the producer told me this I began to calm down, I thought she wanted me just to call in my story.

Then the producer asked me if I can be there tomorrow. I was thinking in my head, "Why does she want me to be in Chicago when I can just call from my mom's house?" I asked the producer what she meant and the producer replied: "We want you to be a guest on the show." I looked at my tv and saw how bored I was so I replied: "Sure, I have nothing else to do." The producer said she would call me back to tell me the travel plans.

Did I call my mom right away? Umm, no. Instead I called my friend Patty in Connecticut. Her mom answered the phone and I asked Patty's mom what time does the Oprah show come on there? Her mom replied "4 pm." I told Patty's mom to record the show, tape a note on their VCR, telling Patty to watch but don't give the surprise away. Patty's mom agreed and said even if she has to, she'll sit on top of Patty to hold her down and watch.

Then I called my mom. Earlier I said I woke up sick. When I called mom I tried my weakest voice. I said to her, "Mom, you have to take a couple of days off work." My mom asked me if I needed to go to the hospital. I told her "No, because we're going to Chicago." She exclaimed: "We're not going to Chicago just so you can see the Cubs play! I took off work two weeks ago so we could go to the Smokey Mountains!" With as much seriousness I could gather without breaking into a hysterical laugh I said: "Well I guess you're not going to be on the Oprah Winfrey Show with me are you?" Even though she denies it I heard my mom dropped her work phone and when she picked it back up she goes, "What did you say?"

I repeated myself and told her that they've been trying to

get a hold of me for six weeks when finally Kirk's mom gave them the Indianapolis number. My mom accused me of lying.

When my mom came home from work she still didn't believe me. The producer called back to tell me the travel itinerary. I asked the producer if she can tell my mom because my mom thinks I'm making the story up. The producer chuckled and said yes.

I turned the phone over to my mom telling her it's long distance. My mom took down all the information thanked the producer and hung up. All of a sudden my mom turned into a little kid. She literally jumped up and down on the couch saying: "We're going to be on the Oprah Winfrey Show! We're going to be on the Oprah Winfrey Show!"

Then just as quickly, my mom stopped and said, "We have to cancel." I asked why? My mom replied, "The tv cameras makes you look ten pounds heavier, plus I need to get my hair done, buy a new outfit, get my nails done, lose weight. I can't do all of that in less than two days." I told my mom we're not cancelling just because of that. This is my big break. I dreamt about it just the night before.

So we started calling everyone we knew to tell them about this. My friends of course were very skeptical. I just said watch Wednesday and you'll see.

Tuesday, August 7th. Heading to the airport, I told my mom, "let me do the talking." Since I was the guest, I felt it was my responsibility. We get to the airport, go up to the counter and I said to the clerk. "Two round trip tickets please to Chicago under the name Kent Bell." The clerk responded: "That'll be $564 apiece." My mom naturally started flipping out. I calmly said to the clerk, "Excuse me but I think they're already paid for." The clerk looked at his computer and said: "Oh, you're going to be on the Oprah Winfrey Show, Here's your tickets. Have a safe trip." When he said it several people stared at me.

We fly to Chicago. The length of time from Indianapolis to Chicago flight is 32 minutes. Remember that because it comes in handy later on.

When we landed in Chicago, an armed security guard was assigned to me. That's right an armed security guard for me. We pass by a wall of phones. The security guard takes out a small piece of paper with only a phone number on it. She calls the number and says, "He's here." and hangs up. I started to get paranoid about this thinking even before I get on the show somebody's trying to kill me. So I asked the security guard is there anything I need to know? She chuckled and said "No, we do this for all our guests. No matter if you're a celebrity or not we protect you and treat you as if you were a celebrity." First class stuff.

We go outside to wait for my ride. It wasn't a limousine as you normally see. This was a cream colored Mercedes-Benz with all the bling of a limo. The chauffeur helps me into the car. Everybody in the parking area stopped to see me. They thought I was a celebrity Ha!

We start heading to the hotel. Remember I said the flight from Indy to Chicago was 32 minutes? Well, the drive from O'Hare airport to the hotel took 45 minutes. That's right. Flying from Indy to Chicago actually took less time. As we were in downtown Chicago, I decided to have some fun with the locals.

I had my mom roll down my window just a little. Since the windows were heavily tinted, they couldn't see inside. Since my window was slightly opened they could hear what was going on inside. At each stop light I started laughing like Eddie Murphy. The chauffeur was very amused because just a week earlier he was driving Eddie Murphy to the Oprah show. By the third stop light people were shoving pieces of paper for me, er I mean Eddie Murphy to sign.

Instead I would sign my name and mom would stick them back out the window. I heard one person say: "Oh that must be the name Eddie Murphy uses when he wants to be incognito."

We checked into the hotel. We called the producer to see if we're going to have dinner with Oprah. The producer said "no, just go to any of the restaurants in the hotel, order anything you want. Just put your room number on bill sign it and we'll pay for it." So instead of going to the burger place in the hotel my mom and I decided to go to the fancy restaurant. Right away we knew we were in a really fancy restaurant. There were no prices on the menu. It was one of those places if you have to ask how much, you don't belong here, type of restaurants. My mom actually asked me how can we afford it? I said to mom, "Don't worry, Oprah's paying for it." My mom immediately smiled and ordered Pheasant. I ordered Roasted Duck. My mom and I agreed that I had the better meal.

Before ordering my meal, I noticed two women sitting at the table across from us. These women were well dressed, they looked intelligent but one of them couldn't help herself by showing her ignorance. She was practically laying on her table to look under my table to see if I had legs. I pretended that I was praying when actually I could see at the top of my eyes at her.

I told my mom to take away my menu and asked her not to yell at me for what I'm about to do. My mom asked me what was going on. I just repeated, "to take away my menu and asked her not to yell at me for what I'm about to do." She removed the menu. I had my head down as if I was praying. Then suddenly, I jerked my head up and with wild eyes stared back at the woman.

When I stared down the woman she literally melted back into her chair. When I say melted you remember the cartoons where a character would melt unto the floor or chair? Well, that's what I did to this lady.

My mom asked me why I did that. I told her in a voice to where I was loud enough for the woman to hear but at the same time I did not want to be obnoxious myself. I said to my mom. "Look at that lady. She looks like she's sophisticated and intelligent but she was making a fool of herself by staring at me so I had to teach her it's not polite to stare." Mission accomplished.

We finished dinner and went to bed. Because the next day I'm gonna be on national tv. We were told before we left the hotel to pack our bags and bring them to the car. I thought what was the reason? Because after we do the show we go home.

The show at that time was live, only in Chicago at 9 a.m. The first part of the show was dealing with people with disabilities who have negative attitudes about their lives and parents of children with disabilities who literally wanted their child to die.

Then the second part of the show was the positive attitudes. Guess which part I was on.

During the negative part of the show, I was in the "Green room" with two doctors. We were watching the negativity and making jokes. In one instance a parent stated on the show that "There are 27,000,000 Americans without health insurance." One of the doctors in the "Green room" replied: "It's 29,000,000." To which the other doctor quipped: "What's a couple of million?"

Right before my segment, the producer came in grabbed my wheelchair and says "you're next."

Because of my illness and the short time between them

calling me and doing the show, I had no time for preparation or stage fright until…

When the producer pushed me into the studio we were behind the audience. I was looking to the stage through the tv camera's viewfinder. Oprah leads into the commercial break with this statement: "Next we will meet a man with no arms or legs who is happy to live."

That's when it hit me. I thought Crap! She's talking about me. Since the show was live in Chicago we only had 90 seconds to push me on stage, sitting me next to Oprah, putting the microphone on me, making sure my shirt and hair were not messed up. As they were putting the microphone on me Oprah asks me how I felt? I replied: "To tell you the truth, I'm scared as hell." Yes, I cursed at Oprah. She was very nice and said: "You'll be fine."

There was a part in the show where Oprah asks me if I felt people who have disabilities are negative are just having a pity party. I answered yes. When I said that, the camera did a closeup on one of the guests. It looked as if she wanted to slap me in the head.

After the show finished, all of the guests went into the green room. I of course was far away from the girl who looked like she wanted to slap me.

Oprah sat in a chair and thanked the audience individually for coming. That, my friends, is a class act.

Then Oprah came into the room and talked to us. The first person was me. She went all the way to the far end of the room just to talk to me first. She thanked me and said I did great. Then we got into our cars went to the airport and flew home. By the time we got home it was 1:00 p.m. The show came on at 4:00 so I took a nap. Then at 4:00, through the magic of television, I was both in Chicago and Indianapolis at the same time.

It was strange watching myself from my own living room and telling my mom, wow just a few hours ago we were over 200 miles away and now here we are back home watching ourselves.

That whole week, month, year was a complete blur. I had to go back to school. When I got there you would have thought I was king of Lexington. Everybody wanted my autograph, or just say hi. Two funny situations happened due to my new found popularity.

I was at a campus bus stop waiting for the shuttle. Two girls were walking towards the bus stop and were pointing at me. When they got there one of the girls asked me if I was on Donahue. I told her no. She insisted she saw me on Phil Donahue. After a couple of minutes of back and forth, I finally said: "Look, I know what show I was on. I was on the Oprah Winfrey Show." She then asked me if I could do her a favor. She was in freshman composition class. She had an assignment to write a report on a famous person, and she picked me.

I was honored but I told her, I'm not rich and famous. I was just on that one show. She replied: "That's good enough for me because you are here and I can actually talk to you." So we scheduled a time to meet so she can interview me. A couple of weeks later she sees me, runs to me gives me a big hug. She thanked me because her report got an A.

The next funny situation was with the Wheelchair basketball team the UK Wheelkats. In 1989 we were very, very good. We went undefeated in conference play and lost only two regular season games and made the playoffs.

One reason we were so good was because of a dashing young stud from Australia named Tim. Even though he was only 19, he knew how to maneuver his chair like a ballroom dancer. He could do everything. Shoot, pass, dribble, play defense and if needed sell popcorn.

One evening our team was putting on an exhibition in Cincinnati, Ohio. Tim was doing his best imitation of Harlem Globetrotter great Meadowlark Lemon. He was dribbling around the other team as if they were the New York Generals.

He was going into the crowd, talking to people and just having fun.

After the exhibition, the team would line up and talk to the fans. Since Tim was the young cute funny guy he naturally had the most people. Until…a kid in my line, who was approximately 7 years old with blonde hair came closer to me. He made my day when he walked up to me, and softly asked: "Excuse me sir but were you on the Oprah Winfrey Show?"

# 22

## Nephews and Nieces

*The Fabulous Four-Jennifer, Kent, Christopher and Mitch Bell*

I owe Christopher a lot. In 2001 he moved to Florida to be my attendant until I could get this Medicaid straightened out. He prevented me from going into a nursing home or moving to Georgia where there's nothing to do. Thank you Christopher. I love you

# 23

## Kent and Sherri's Interview

Kent: What was your first reaction (if any) when you saw me in Spanish class?

Sherri: I guess I could say I was caught off guard. I hadn't met anyone without arms and legs.

Kent: What did you think when Mr. Hulce drafted you to be my pusher to my next class?

Sherri: That was okay. I was able to get out of class early, which was always good.

Kent: What was it like for those two years you were pushing me around class?

Sherri: I had a wonderful time with you. We always had fun. We got along from the very beginning. You were very funny and I was not, but you laughed at my jokes anyway. After awhile, I didn't really even think about you not being able to walk, etc. We just became friends and I didn't really think about it. You offered so much to any situation. You were always the life of the party. What I liked was the fact that we could talk to each other about anything. Overall we had a great time. Do you remember my books? You carried them on your lap and you would always lean forward and dump them out when we were joking around.

Kent: What have I taught you during our friendship?

Sherri: Here is what have you taught me? That no matter what you are dealt in life you can deal with it. Even though people aren't nice sometimes, it's their problem, doesn't need to be yours. No one is any better than anyone else. Just because you may not have something someone else does, doesn't mean you are not important and don't belong at the top of your game. Fight for what you believe in. And keep your friends and family close.

<u>Sherri's comments</u>. After high school what was it like when we went out? I have to tell you, and I know we have discussed this, it was when I came to your house to see you after high school, I think it was after you were on the Oprah show. Your mom

greeted me at the door (sweet as always) invited me in and you came rolling toward me. You weren't in your wheelchair and you didn't have your legs or arms on. I was used to seeing you without your arms, but I had never seen you without your legs. I don't know why it surprised me so much, but it did. Your mom saw the look on my face and you both laughed, then I laughed and that was it. I enjoyed the times we went to dinner or even when we were able to see each other for a while to catch up, Meeting your friends at your apt.

Kent: Can you remember any funny stories/situations?

Sherri: Well, with you that's easy. The first story that comes to mind is when we left spanish and you were smarting off to me so I pushed you in the girls bathroom and you tried to use your head against the door opening so I wouldn't be able to do it. You were playing swords (or whatever you call it) with Greg in spanish with pencils. When you tried to wear your new arms and they went wild grabbing and swinging (or at least you said it was a malfunction, we'll never know:)) Will we?

I think you are a wonderful person and I am so glad you came into my life. I'm glad we have been able to keep in touch after all these years. You have taught me so many valuable lessons. I am never surprised to hear you are trying something new... like skiing. Oh my gosh, I can't do that well. But I have to tell you if I was there the day you were skiing, I would have flipped you over into the water. Oh, I'm sorry, did I say that out loud, that's for all the times you picked on me over the years:0) Love ya and miss not seeing you. Glad you have come into all our lives. We are truly blessed to have you.

Love Sherri

# 24

## Thank You

In closing, you cannot tell me there is no such thing as a loving kind God. As mentioned in my chapter about my father accepting Jesus and having Jesus use me to guide my dad to accepting him and in the Hand of God chapter I have experienced God's love and mercy first hand. Also, how can anyone explain how I have defied the odds of living as long as I have and being successful at it?

I'll tell you how. God Almighty. He blessed me with being born in the only family who was strong enough to handle the situation. He has blessed me with wonderful friends in helping me along when my family wasn't close enough.

He has blessed me by guiding me in directions where I might not want to go but it was in God's best interest. Finally, he has blessed me by being my savior and giving me grace to do the things he wants me to do.

So to all who says there is no God…. I say there is and I'm a living rolling example of his love.

Thank you.
KENT

Co-Author:
Bobbie Jean Yates Chestnut
Author of "WHEW" HOW DID I EVER DO IT?